Spartacus

A Captivating Guide to the Thracian Gladiator Who Led the Slave Rebellion Called the Third Servile War against the Roman Republic

Free Bonus from Captivating History (Available for a Limited time)

Hi History Lovers!

Now you have a chance to join our exclusive history list so you can get your first history ebook for free as well as discounts and a potential to get more history books for free! Simply visit the link below to join.

Captivatinghistory.com/ebook

Also, make sure to follow us on Facebook, Twitter and Youtube by searching for Captivating History.

Contents

Introduction

Almost 2,100 years ago, a gladiator walked out of the arena. And he never walked back into it.

Spartacus, a Thracian whose early life is hidden in the mists of history, is one of the most infamous figures of antiquity. Perhaps the most famous gladiator of all, parts of Spartacus' story inspired elements of the award-winning film *Gladiator* (2000). Yet even though his story is familiar to millions, he remains a strangely mysterious figure, one whose innermost heart was never revealed to the world. All of the existing records about Spartacus and the war that he started and lost were written by Roman historians. None of the slaves' account of these events has survived the onslaught of the years; thus, many of Spartacus' actions, and all of his motives, are matters of speculation. Even Plutarch, a contemporary, could only guess at what this hero of the oppressed truly wanted or how he really felt. Diving into this great man's psyche and puzzling together his thoughts and feelings is a fascinating subject. And his story makes for gripping reading.

Born a free man—possibly even a prince—he had become a mercenary for the Romans. Then he'd been a deserter, a bandit, and an insurgent. When they caught him, he became a prisoner. And then they sold him as a slave.

At the so-called "school" (really more of a prison) at Capua, Spartacus became a gladiator. All his life, he had known how to fight for food, resources, and survival. Now, the Romans forced him to fight for their entertainment. It was either fight his fellow slaves or die at their blades, and *fight or die* became the single rule by which Spartacus' life was lived. Shackled at night in a dark and lonely cell and participating by day in a blood sport that could kill him at any second, always at the whim of his master, Spartacus had become one of the most miserable slaves in history.

He lived a slave, but he would die a hero.

With kitchen knives and sheer guts and determination, Spartacus and a handful of his friends would fight their way out of the school at Capua and go in search of a better life. And so, their journey began, a journey that has captivated the imaginations of millions, from Marxist revolutionaries to novelists and filmmakers. Now, allow Spartacus' story to capture yours.

This story has all the hallmarks of a tale more exciting than history, a tale that comes to life with the excitement of fiction and yet the poignant reality of true events. There are battles and consuls, Romans and Thracians, slaves and the free. There are pirates and gladiators, as well as a jealous praetor seeking to prove himself in the eyes of the public, pitted against a courageous freedom fighter whose only goal is to get back to his homeland. Treachery, greed, power, freedom, ingenuity, and imagination fill this tale, which takes place all the way from the feet of Vesuvius to the mighty rampart of the Alps to the shores of the Strait of Messina.

This is the story of Spartacus. And this book will bring it to you as you've never heard it before.

Chapter 1 – Thrace and Its Enemies

The story of Thrace begins long before history, in the mysterious darkness of a time when writing had not yet been invented. That era is long lost to us, but that is not to say that it was uneventful. People were people then just as they are now, and as now, they were busy: making war, obtaining nourishment, falling in love, searching for a place to call home. And around eight thousand years ago, somewhere around 6000 BCE, a group of Indo-European tribes stumbled upon a land that their people would call home for the next six millennia. Bound by mountains to the east, a great river to the north, and seas on the south and east, this land was one of wild and abundant beauty. Its cascading rivers had carved for themselves great harsh valleys, the landscape plunging down into the roaring expanse of the river. The mountains ran down into great plateaus as wide and wild as the mighty sky, and the seas were glittering blue, warm to the touch, awash with natural resources. With damp, cool winters and hot, dry summers, this land appeared perfect to the tribes who found themselves wandering into its untamed wilderness.

The land was a part of modern-day Bulgaria, Turkey, and Greece, known to history as Thrace, and the peoples who first came to live there were known as the proto-Thracians. They were a group of agricultural tribes who tilled the fertile earth and raised animals on the rich grazing lands, and soon, this little handful of people grew up into a vast nation. "Thrace" was not their own name for their country. In fact, what the Thracians called themselves has been lost to the mists of time; the name was bestowed upon them by the Greeks.

But for thousands of years, the Greeks stayed in Greece, and the Thracians of Thrace were free to explore and tend to their crops and animals in the rich abundance of their beautiful surroundings. Most of what we know about Thracian culture comes from archaeological findings; the first written record of Thrace is a vague reference in Homer's *Iliad*, and it was only in 450 BCE that Herodotus would thoroughly document these people. It would appear, however, that despite their simple lives in small rural villages, the Thracians had a rich and fascinating culture. They loved poetry and music, although none of it survived to this day. They were also polygamists and believed in the afterlife, having elaborate burial sites and rituals.

To all appearances, the Thracians thrived. And lacking any oppressor to force them into unity, they began to squabble with one another. As the centuries slipped by, the Thracians continued to make war among themselves. These wars made their young men strong and nimble, developing weapons and armor that was unrivaled among the neighboring countries and regions. Living in villages instead of cities, these men became outstanding guerilla warriors as they fought each other, relying on their sharp wits, knowledge of the landscape, and excellent equipment. The Thracians carried crescent-shaped wicker shields, javelins, and a large dagger known as a *sica*, which was made of steel. They were quick on their feet and mobile, moving effortlessly through the rugged landscape to wage war on each other over land, resources, and power.

Historians have reflected that it was a pity the Thracians chose to pit themselves against each other instead of against the neighboring Greeks and Macedonians. Such was their military prowess that they may well have been able to conquer their neighbors and build an empire of their own. Instead, every time a threat arose from beyond their borders, the Thracians were too busy fighting each other to stand against their enemies as one united force. The Thracians could probably have beaten anyone in a war if they had only been able to bring themselves to peace. But they never did.

Around 700 BCE, the ancient Greeks began to colonize Thrace fairly peacefully. The Greeks became a profound influence on Thrace and its people, and they also became the first people to write about the Thracians, describing them as fearless fighters. Greek armies at the time were largely made up of hoplites, slow-moving foot soldiers burdened with heavy spears and shields. Greek generals decided that the Thracians would be ideal additions to their army, and so, they hired thousands of them as mercenaries. These mercenaries became known as peltasts.

In the early 6th century BCE, Persia, under King Darius the Great, swept across the Balkans and attacked. The Thracians could not find the unity to fight them, and as such, their country was incorporated into the mighty Achaemenid Persian Empire. Darius made their soldiers a vital part of his conquests, and they were wildly successful. With the help of the Thracians, he conquered most of Europe and almost all of Thrace, expanding his empire all the way to the shores of the Black Sea. It should be noted that while some Thracian tribes joined Darius, others decided to stand against him; these forces were annihilated.

But the Persian Empire, despite Darius' brilliance as a commander, was a shooting star: staggering while it lasted but very brief. The Achaemenid Empire went into decline after his rule, and in the 5th century BCE, Thrace made one great attempt to stand together. Forty of its two hundred tribes came together to build a kingdom known as the Odrysian Kingdom, and for a brief and wonderful period, the world was given a glimpse of what Thrace could have been. It became a much larger territory and grew in power to the point that Thracians now hired Greek mercenaries, with the heavy hoplites complementing the quick peltasts. Xenophon, the famed Greek writer and historian, was one of them.

The Odrysian Kingdom was mighty, but a man arose who was mightier still: Alexander the Great. His father, Philip II, was the first Macedonian who made a mostly successful bid to conquer Thrace; Alexander finished the job in the spring of 335 BCE, and the Odrysian Kingdom was obliterated. Thrace would never again find the unity that had given it almost a century of power. The people that had been conquerors were now merely conquests, with the victorious army broken up and hired out as mercenaries for the Macedonians.

Macedonia's great enemy thus became Thrace's great enemy, and like those that had gone before, this new power would be quick to use Thrace's human resources. This power was ancient Rome—the late Roman Republic, to be exact (it would only become an empire in the first century BCE). At the Battle of Pydna in 168 BCE, Macedonia and Rome faced off against one another. It was a terrible defeat for Macedonia, despite their superior numbers. Rome butchered about 31,000 out of their 43,000 men; by contrast, only 100 Romans fell that day. Macedonia's power was no more, and Rome slowly began to occupy Thrace.

Rome had been in existence for hundreds of years, and since the beginning, slaves had been a part of the city and its growing territories. There was hardly a part of Rome's famed culture that was not built on the backs of men and women who worked without rights, without wages, and without justice. They were in every industry: public works, war, manufacturing, farming, and mining. Mining was among the worst. Trapped in suffocating darkness, their way lit only by the smoky and flickering glow cast by torches, these slaves were left to dig through the hearts of mountains like helpless worms.

Some of the slaves who lived in sumptuous luxury in Roman palaces had it far worse than even the miners, however. Sex slaves, many of them children, abounded in Rome. For these children, molestation was a daily occurrence, and some would be castrated.

Even the poorest of Romans could afford a slave or two, with the rich owning hundreds. Many of these slaves had been born in their masters' homes, as the child of a slave woman was, by default, a slave as well. Others were procured through more violent means. Prisoners of war, except for those of the highest status, automatically became slaves. Those who were unable to pay their debts would also be enslaved, and very poor families would sometimes sell their own children into slavery.

The most notorious source of slaves was piracy. While the pirates of the Caribbean may have been immortalized in film, the pirates of the ancient Mediterranean were hardly any less fearsome. Under Rome's very nose, they harried the surrounding shores, making their homes close to or even within Roman territory. At the time of Roman Thrace, these pirates inhabited western Cilicia, on the southern coast of modern-day Turkey. And they ran rampant. Stealing, killing, and kidnapping at will, these pirates could have been crushed within Rome's iron fist at any time—except they weren't. Rome needed them. The truth was that these Cilician pirates captured thousands of slaves each year and brought them to Italy to be sold cheaply. Piracy was Rome's most readily available source of slaves, and as long as the Cilician pirates supplied slaves to feed the insatiable appetite for human resources that belonged to a growing power, they would be allowed to wreak havoc in relative peace.

While the Roman Empire had an overwhelming number of slaves, it was the Roman Republic in which they suffered the most. Here, slaves were a dime a dozen, thanks to the overwhelming number of wars that Rome was waging with the Gauls, Britons, and Parthians, to name but a few. The influx of prisoners of war was more than enough to keep Rome supplied with slaves, and because they were so cheap, their masters treated them brutally. What did it matter if a slave died? They could be easily replaced.

Culturally, slaves were so much a part of the Roman world that their presence—and, in the Roman Republic, the harsh treatment of them—was wholly unquestioned. It would only be many years later that slaves would become a contentious issue; in the 2nd century BCE, they were simply a matter of fact. Roman thinking had molded itself so completely around slavery that it would never be questioned. In fact, it would only end when the Roman Empire itself fell in the 8th century CE.

Some of the slaves, however, did aspire for a better life. It is hard to imagine that any of them wouldn't; even those living in luxury were subject to their master's every whim. Yet it was only rarely that they would take action on a large scale, resulting in what became known as the Servile Wars.

The first two Servile Wars took place within forty years of one another. The first, taking place between 135 and 132 BCE, was led by Eunus, a Scythian slave who claimed to receive visions from the gods. In a Joan of Arc-esque uprising, he rallied tens of thousands of slaves in Sicily and attempted to build a city and state of his own. For three years, it looked as though he would succeed, but the Roman army eventually conquered Eunus' army and dragged him off to prison, where illness claimed his life.

The Second Servile War, which took place between 104 and 103 BCE, also took place in Sicily. Consul Gaius Marius had around 800 Italian slaves of the region freed, which sowed discontent among non-Italian slaves, causing them to rise up against their masters. Salvius, who was also a slave, decided to make a bid for what Eunus had come so close to achieving. He led thousands of well-armed troops against Rome, yet his attempt was even shorter-lived. Marius' successors, Quintus Servilius Caepio and Gaius Atilius Serranus, put a stop to the revolt within a year, but it was no easy task.

Yet despite the Servile Wars, there was no question in Roman minds that slavery was simply a part of their culture and would never be changed. So, the pillaging of human freedom went on, with hundreds of thousands of slaves daily carrying out the wills of their masters, their voices drowned out, their faces forgotten.

Rome's consuls and emperors might be some of the most familiar names in history, but it was regiments of slaves who built their empire. Most of these slaves were nameless and faceless, their identities lost forever as irrelevant.

All except for one. And his name was Spartacus.

Chapter 2 – On the Romans' Side

Little is known about the early life of one of history's greatest heroes. The Thracians did not keep much in the way of written records, and they certainly did not keep any records of who could possibly have been a rather inconsequential young man who was born among them. He may have been from the Maedi tribe, a Thracian group known for their nomadic ways. It is vaguely possible that he may have been of royal blood; however, it is more likely that he lived like the majority of the other Thracians had been doing for centuries: in a rural village, roaming the vast plains and rocky crags of his country, tending to livestock.

Even Spartacus' birth year is utterly unknown, although we know he was still a fairly young and definitely very physically capable man when he died in 71 BCE. The estimate most generally accepted for his birth year is 111 BCE, which would have made him about forty when he died.

But that death was a long way away—and practically unimaginable—for the young Spartacus who lived in the land of his ancestors. Roman oppression was as rife in Thrace as anywhere, and as he grew, the young man became more and more aware of what was happening to his people. Just as the Romans were unable to make the crags of the Balkans bow down to them, there was something in the spirit of the Thracians that conquering armies could not extinguish. And it was nowhere stronger than in the heart of Spartacus.

Still, there was little he could do about it, no matter how much it chafed at him that the Romans dictated how his people lived and hired thousands of them to fight their wars. Young and unsure of his future, Spartacus did what most young Thracian men were doing at the time: he joined the Roman military.

There are no records to indicate where Spartacus served or even in which capacity, although due to his lack of Roman citizenship, he would not have served as a legionary. Classical sources mention only the fact that he was a Roman soldier; he was more than likely a mercenary, as most Thracians were, serving in the Auxilia (the auxiliary troops that complemented the much-famed Roman legions). Just as the Greeks had hired the light-footed Thracians to complement their lumbering hoplites, the Romans found these fleet and agile soldiers useful when partnered with their slow legions. Still, one can surmise that Spartacus was a fairly gifted young warrior and that he may have been given some form of command. It was in the Roman army—the army that had conquered vast swathes of the known world—that Spartacus began to learn the art of war. And he learned it well. Thrace had taught him how to fight— warrior's blood coursed through the veins of all young Thracian men—and Rome put that fighting to good work. Spartacus got his first taste of the thrill of hot blood and cold steel meeting, and he also began to learn how to command a group of men, if only by observing how he himself was being commanded. He learned much, and the knowledge would later serve him well. But Roman discipline did not sit well with the Thracian fire in Spartacus' blood.

While Spartacus tried to learn how to balance both fire and steel, hundreds of miles away in Rome, a young man named Marcus Licinius Crassus watched as his family shattered around him.

The political climate of Rome in the early 80s BCE was a stormy one. The Republic of Rome was dying in the childbirth of the Roman Empire. Its unique system of government had served it well for hundreds of years, but the bloated territory was growing too vast to be controlled by consuls. It needed a single, unifying leader whose word was law, but it would still be decades before Julius Caesar became that leader. For now, political intrigue and violence, frequently bordering on civil war, would become rife.

Marcus Licinius Crassus, whether he liked it or not, had been dragged into the mess of Roman politics. Born in 115 BCE, Crassus was raised simply but with an abundant awareness of the power surrounding him. His parents lived in a small home with only a few slaves and no ostentatious displays of power, yet power was something with which the family was very familiar. Crassus' father, Publius Licinius Crassus Dives, was one of Rome's most important figures and a leading military commander, as well as a highly capable and respected politician. When Marcus was only eighteen, Publius had become consul, the highest position that could be held in the Roman Republic; he also served as a commander in modern-day Spain. As Marcus entered adulthood, and despite Publius' and his mother's attempts to raise him thriftily, he learned more than just an acquaintance with power. He learned arrogance.

Marcus' pride would come before a fall. In 88 and 87 BCE, when he was in his late twenties, Rome experienced an upheaval that would change Crassus' life.

From 91 to 88 BCE, Rome had experienced yet another civil war, known as the Social War, when governor Marcus Livius Drusus the Younger intended to grant Roman citizenship to Roman allies living in Italy, which would have tipped the balance of power harshly away from the Roman nobility. His assassination caused the Roman Republic to erupt into civil war. Gaius Marius, who had been a consul six times and was one of the most ambitious men in Rome, intended to lead the fight against Italy; however, the Senate saw fit to send Lucius Cornelius Sulla Felix instead. Sulla proved to be an outstanding commander, who led Rome to a brisk victory against Italy, and as much as Marius was on the winning side, the victory to him felt more like a defeat. Sulla had proven himself to be Rome's darling, and Marius felt his power was being threatened.

Thus, the battle cries of the Social War of 91-88 BCE had barely begun to fade when they began anew, this time in Sulla's War, which lasted between 88 and 87 BCE. Sulla was determined to grab more power, as his military command had naturally led into a political career. Marius, on the other hand, was extravagantly ambitious, and it is perhaps fitting with Publius' personality that he chose to back Sulla instead. Marcus Crassus joined his father in supporting Sulla, and for a few months, it appeared that they had made the right choice. Marius, then holding more political power, had Sulla kicked out of Rome. However, the slighted general returned with several well-disciplined legions of his own and did the unthinkable: he marched within the city's bounds and meant to attack Rome itself. In all the civil wars the Roman Republic had faced, this move was considered to be unspeakably cruel. Marius had not expected his adversary to deal him so low a blow. He had only a ragtag bunch of gladiators to defend the city, and they fell before Sulla's legions. Sulla took power and became a Roman consul, sending Marius fleeing for his life.

But Marius did not stay down for long. Finding refuge only as far away as distant North Africa, where he fought in the Jugurthine War between Rome and Numidia (modern-day Algeria), Marius began to drum up support thanks to his victory, and it was not a difficult task. Sulla's unethical decision to attack the city of Rome had shaken even his supporters, although Publius and Crassus remained loyal.

Driven by a long-ago prophecy that he would become a consul of Rome seven times, Marius was determined to return to Rome and receive his grandiose fate. He was able to put together a more powerful army and marched on Rome just as Sulla had done—and he was even more brutal in his treatment of Sulla's supporters. Over a hundred Roman nobles were butchered for their loyalty to Sulla, and their heads were paraded around the Roman Forum for all to see.

For Rome, this was another wound inflicted on their Republic that was fast being torn apart. For Publius and Crassus, it was a life-changing disaster. Crassus had known little other than stability throughout his young life; now, all of that was going to be uprooted. Publius was found to have supported Sulla, and he was forced to kill himself. Crassus' brother was simply killed. And Crassus had no choice: he had to flee, or he would suffer a similar fate.

His family killed, his home life stripped away from him, and even his pride trampled under the marching feet of Marius' army, Crassus fled like a kicked dog. The only place he could think to go was back to Spain, a long and grueling journey for a young man who had never known want, but at least there he found people who had been his father's allies during his governorship there. They took him in, finding a hiding place for him in a cave by the sea.

So, this was how the 80s BCE found two young men who would someday become the bloodiest of enemies. One, fleet-footed young Spartacus of Thrace, serving in the Roman army and getting his first taste of battle. The other, arrogant Marcus Licinius Crassus of Rome, hiding in a cave overlooking the beating waves. And as Spartacus grew to dislike the Roman legions that had persecuted his people more and more, Crassus gazed out over the foaming sea, alone and afraid. And bitterness grew thick and black in both their hearts.

Chapter 3 – Sold

Illustration I: A contemporary bust of Marcus Licinius Crassus

For eight long months, Crassus sat in that cave, experiencing heat and cold, day and night through the rocky mouth that offered him a view of the ever-changing sea. And in those eight months—fed and watered by an ally who discreetly sent provisions to him every day—Crassus learned about himself. He learned about how much he missed his father. He learned about how badly hardship suited him. And he learned that he never wanted to experience such loneliness, discomfort, and exile ever again.

Meanwhile, Spartacus was probably serving in the Roman army around this time (it is impossible to be certain when exactly he joined, as history's timeline of Spartacus only begins at 73 BCE). But he wouldn't serve for long. He, too, was learning—and mostly what he was learning was that he hated Rome with a fervent passion. Whether he had joined the army for the money or because an honorable discharge would lead to a Roman citizenship and all the privileges that came with it, it was no longer worth it to Spartacus. Something about the Romans must have chafed at him. Maybe it was their history of exploiting Thracians to fight their wars for him. Maybe it was the uncreative discipline of their armies, marching in unison to conquer the world. History cannot tell us of his motives, but for whatever reason, there came a time when Spartacus had abruptly had enough.

So, he did the unthinkable. He deserted.

Deserters were dealt with harshly in Roman times. In fact, most were lucky to simply be banished, their titles and possessions stripped from them as they were driven from the land to fend for themselves. Most were killed, sometimes being clubbed brutally to death by their own comrades once they were captured. Spartacus knew that he was risking death by leaving the Roman ranks, but he decided that living as a free Thracian instead of as a Roman pawn was worth it. In fact, he detested the Romans so much that he became a thorn in their side throughout their expeditions in Thrace and elsewhere, harassing his erstwhile comrades. Some sources say that Spartacus even began to rally support against the Romans from among his own people, working as an insurgent. Others say that he was simply a bandit, attacking the legions to carry off their wealth. It does not seem impossible, given the events that later followed, for the former to have been true. Spartacus had the charisma and the charm necessary to start a rebellion. In fact, if he had been allowed to do this, it is possible that history might have seemed very different. Perhaps if Spartacus had been able to truly rally and unify the wayward Thracians, if he could get them to stand behind his banner and fight the Romans, then Thrace might exist to this day.

But Spartacus never got the chance. His rebellion, if there even was one, never got off the ground because his luck ran out before he could get any further. The Romans captured him once again.

It's not clear why Spartacus wasn't executed for his crime, but his physique likely had something to do with it. The Thracians were a hard and warlike race to start with; Spartacus had been fighting either with or against the greatest army in the world for months. He was mightily strong, a tall figure with rippling muscles that rivaled those of any Roman soldier. Their numbers had overwhelmed him, but they recognized his prowess. Perhaps motivated by money, the Roman commander who had captured Spartacus at last elected not to kill him. He was worth nothing dead, but sold into slavery, Spartacus could make his captor rich.

And so, like Joseph at the hands of his brothers, Spartacus was sold into slavery by the men who had fought alongside him, the men he had left behind. His great strength made him ideally suited to a specific niche in the world of Roman slaves. Spartacus' fate did not include hefting great weights in construction, swinging a pick in a dark mine, or carrying sacks of flour on a mill or farm. Instead, he would do what he had always done. He would fight.

Spartacus became a gladiator.

The Roman gladiator's origins lay beyond Rome itself, back in the distant past when the majority of Italy was populated by a people known as the Etruscans. It was the Etruscans themselves, in fact, who pressured the village of Rome into becoming a place of unity for the tribes they oppressed, thus growing it into a mighty kingdom. After a time, the Etruscans had joined Rome, with some even becoming kings of it before the Roman Republic was born. Thus, Rome had a strong Etruscan influence on its culture, and perhaps one of the most famous of these influences is the gladiator.

The Etruscans, unlike the Romans, did not use warrior-slaves for entertainment. Instead, they were a part of the Etruscan religion, where they were likely involved with death rites. In fact, when the gladiatorial games first occurred in Rome, they were also a part of the funeral rites of distinguished men. Dozens of slaves belonging to the deceased would fight to the death in a messy and brutal melee as a way of honoring the memory of the warlike dead. The first recorded instance of these slave fights at a funeral occurred in the 3rd century BCE. By the 1st century BCE, these fights were no longer part of the morbid. They were simply entertainment for Rome's yammering masses.

As cultured as Rome could be in its plays, poetry, and music, its entertainment could also be utterly barbaric—and nothing was more so than the gladiatorial games. Gladiators were slaves trained for fighting, and in front of crowds that numbered in the thousands, they would be pitted against one another for the bloodthirsty enjoyment of the audience. While not all the games ended in death, serious injury and mortality were nonetheless very common. And even though the gladiators became to the people of ancient Rome what celebrities are to the modern world, they were still classed as the lowest of the low, with no basic rights and no freedom.

Spartacus had worked with the Romans for long enough to know that this was the fate that awaited him, yet perhaps he was unprepared for the suffering he would endure to get there.

Spartacus was sold to a Roman named Gnaeus Cornelius Lentulus Batiatus, who owned and ran a gladiatorial school in Capua, near modern-day Naples. Little is known about the kind of man that Batiatus was. While the words "gladiator school" conjure up a Hogwarts-esque image with Batiatus as a Dumbledore-like figure, nothing could be further from the truth. This so-called school was no place of wonder and magic: instead, it was little more than a prison. Batiatus and other gladiator trainers like him sought not to empower their gladiators but to make money out of them. A good gladiator was worth a fortune to their owners, and so—physically, anyway—they were well cared for. Fed on fortifying barley to build muscle tone and given only the very best in medical attention, the gladiators were in excellent shape. But they were kept in tiny cells. And, mindful of their physical capabilities and warrior training, their owners kept them in shackles.

For Spartacus, it must have been utterly intolerable. He was not the first Thracian gladiator, nor would he be the last, but like those who had gone before and those who would follow, his heart yearned for the wide skies of Thrace where he had stridden so freely only months before. His wife, classically recorded as a prophetess, had been taken from him. His freedom was gone. All he had now was a dark little cell, with fear and despair radiating off the other gladiators around him, and the prospect of grueling training sessions each morning. Should he refuse to cooperate, he would be whipped or maybe burned with a hot iron—but not badly. Oh, never badly enough to damage the physical body of such a fine specimen of a gladiator. Yet everything about the gladiator school was designed to break his spirit.

Unluckily for Rome, they would soon find that Spartacus' spirit would not be so easy to break.

* * * *

After eight long months in the Spanish cave, news reached Crassus. Gaius Marius had gotten his seventh consulship after all, but he had not enjoyed it for long: he died a short while after receiving the title. Now, Rome was under the control of a Marian consul (supporters of Marius were known as "Marians"), but the passionate fire with which Marius had despised all who supported Sulla had died with him. Crassus was free to escape the cave at last.

He knew better than to go back to Rome just yet, however. Sulla was still alive; in fact, he was campaigning in the east, fighting the First Mithridatic War with the Kingdom of Pontus, wisely staying out of trouble while things settled in Rome. But it was clear to Crassus that Sulla was not done with his attempts to gain power, and Crassus was determined to support him, even if that support had cost his father his life. The death of Publius had fixed Marius and his allies once and for all in Crassus' mind as tyrants. He was going to change that.

Luckily for Crassus, he had plenty of influence on his side in Spain, as many of those subjects were loyal to Publius regardless of who governed Rome. Crassus began to amass wealth and loyalty, aiming to build an army that would eventually march in support of Sulla.

Five years after the death of Publius, in 82 BCE, Crassus finally got to flex his new power. Sulla had emerged from the First Mithridatic War as the decisive victor in 85 BCE and decided it was now time to act. He wrote to the Senate, demanding to be allowed to return home and threatening to do it by force if his request was not granted. The consuls at the time—Marian loyalists named Gnaeus Papirius Carbo and Gaius Marius the Younger, Marius' son—marched to meet him in 82 BCE, and Sulla knew it was time to launch his second civil war. Crassus recognized his chance as well. He took his army and marched to meet Sulla, and he and his men played a vital part in the ensuing battle, which would finally turn the tide. Carbo and Cinna were defeated, and Sulla marched to Rome as its new leader.

The feeling of power and victory were dizzying and wonderful to Crassus. He was no longer a young man, but he had still proven himself in battle against Rome's very best. Even better, Sulla began to purge Rome of Marian loyalists, and their confiscated wealth was distributed among Sulla's favorite allies. Crassus, of course, was among them. His wealth grew enormously, and not only thanks to Sulla's handouts. Crassus made a name for himself as an astute—and often unethical—businessman. Amassing real estate for low prices (often as the result of a tragedy, such as a fire), Crassus would sell it again for a much greater amount of money. The sound of gold clinking into his coffers proved to be intoxicating to him. Crassus had a reputation for being both generous and extravagant, and he began to prove himself to be dedicated to growing his wealth at all costs. Taking advantage of someone else's tragedy or naivete was his favorite tactic. He was an excellent public speaker and a conniving flatterer, but at his heart, this smooth-talking businessman hid a selfish core.

It was also during his time serving Sulla that Crassus stumbled upon a whole new vice: jealousy. Popular as he was with Sulla, Crassus was not his greatest darling. That title belonged to a young man by the name of Gnaeus Pompeius Magnus, better known as Pompey the Great. Of course, when he and Crassus first got to know each other, Pompey did not yet bear the title of "Magnus" or "Great." It was clear that Pompey was on his way to greatness, though: talented as Crassus was as a military strategist, Pompey far outshone him. That fact chafed hard at Crassus, and where he might otherwise have been content with his money and power, Crassus began to chase after something he lacked: a tremendous military victory. And just like with money, he would stop at nothing to get it.

Chapter 4 – The Real Gladiator

The roar of the crowd was deafening. Spartacus, waiting in the dark, could feel the ground beneath his feet reverberate with the bellowing approval of the Roman crowd. It made his stomach turn. One can imagine that this could have been one of the things he'd hated most about the Roman legionaries who were once his comrades: the thoughtless bloodlust. He could hear the screams out there in the middle of the arena, knew that people were being butchered, people who didn't ask to fight—people who didn't ask to die.

Spartacus hefted his short, angled sword. Its keen edge could part muscle and bone; he'd seen it happen before, watched as skin peeled back from gleaming flesh. Killing was nothing new to him. He was a soldier, after all. But back in the war zone, killing hadn't been accompanied by the roar of the crowd. And the men whose lives he'd taken hadn't been slaves just like him.

It was time to go. Spartacus took a deep breath, shifting the small, rectangular shield on his arm. Some of the other gladiators tried to hang back, fear in their eyes despite the rigorous training they'd all undergone, training that had left scars on their skin. The trainer and his assistants were ready for them, though: waving red-hot irons and swinging whips, they drove the reluctant slaves toward the arena.

Spartacus was a man of war, and he still had his pride to hold on to. He ignored the trainer and walked into the arena of his own accord. When he stepped into the sunlight, it sparkled on the powerful curves of his shoulders and biceps, the defined lines of his pectorals and abdomen. He wore greaves and padding on his legs, as well as a helmet on his head, the metal catching the sun with a brilliance that made the crowd roar. But his torso and arms were utterly bare. His opponents would be forced to strike there—his chest, ribs, lungs, heart, throat—in order to make things more entertaining for the crowd.

This was no real battle. This was entertainment. Yet it was so much more violent than anything that Spartacus had endured on the battlefield.

There was no time for reflection, though. On the other end of the arena, a heavier champion, this time bearing a massive shield and an arrogant sway, was strutting out on the sand. He was a hoplomachus: a heavily armored mockery of the hoplites that the Thracians had once defeated.

Fittingly, Spartacus was a thraex, or Thracian. Once, real Thracians and real hoplites had clashed on the cold mountainsides of Thrace, and only the scream of the wind in the high peaks had accompanied their battle cries. But now as the hoplomachus hefted his shield and screamed, the whole of Rome screamed with him.

Spartacus didn't want to fight him. But just like his opponent, just like those who'd left nothing but bloodstains and drag marks in the sand, he didn't have a choice.

None of them had a choice.

* * * *

There are no records of any of Spartacus' fights in the gladiatorial arena. While fiction has styled him as one of the best, it is unclear whether he even fought at all, although given his military prowess, it is unlikely that he was a mediocre gladiator. We do know much about the lives of the gladiators in general, however—and for all the glory and honor showered upon them, their lives were far from a bed of roses.

Different classes of gladiators bore different kinds of armor and weapons. The murmillo (also spelled as mirmillo or myrmillo) and the hoplomachus were the most heavily armored, but even they had bare torsos like the thraex. Some, like the retiarius, wore no armor at all and didn't even get to carry a "real" weapon: instead, they had fishing nets and tridents and were pitted against gladiators wearing fish-shaped helmets. Spartacus was more than likely a thraex, considering that he really was Thracian. These light-footed, lightly armored gladiators had to fight the heavy hitters, such as the murmillo.

The fights became more and more organized over the years, reaching a point where they had long sets of rules during the Roman Empire. But in the early days—even in the late Roman Republic—they were still crazy skirmishes, a bloody mess that usually led to death. Reluctant though some of the gladiators may have been, they had no choice but to fight. It was either fight or die. Sometimes they wouldn't even fight other humans; instead, caged animals, starved and goaded into crazed ferocity, would be chased into the arena instead. There was no fleeing a boar or a wolf or a bear on the hunt.

It's uncertain for how long Spartacus was a gladiator. By day, he would have been expected to walk into the arena to the cheers of his adoring fans. If he won, he would be showered in palm leaves and money (which, of course, would go straight to his owner). If he lost, he would be expected to show no fear, even in his dying moment, and to conduct himself always with courageous honor. And by night, he was chained in the dark, kept in a cell, and denied even the right to look up at the stars.

The only bright part of Spartacus' life in the gladiator school was the alliances he managed to forge with his fellow gladiators. During the day, there was no room to talk; there was just training, hours upon hours of it. But at night, when the doors had been bolted and the shackled slaves were left in the darkness, this group of men (and some women) who had been forced to fight for the entertainment of others sought some spark of human contact.

History does not tell us in detail how Spartacus came to know the other gladiators or what their relationships were really like. But considering what came after, their trust in him must have been enormous. Spartacus' radiating charisma, so popular in the gladiatorial arena, did more than simply entertain his fellow slaves outside of it: it inspired them, in a life where inspiration was hard to find. He became well known to the slaves that lived closest to him. Two Gallic gladiators, Crixus and Oenomaus, were particularly close to him. Like Spartacus, they had been taken from wild and beautiful lands that they had once loved and forced to fight in a city they hated. And like Spartacus, they had fire in their blood.

With around 78 gladiators now loyal to Spartacus, the Thracian realized that the time was coming to act. It's uncertain whether Spartacus had plotted a revolt ever since he was first captured or whether life in Capua simply became so unbearable that he saw no other option. Either way, Spartacus made up his mind. He was going to break out of the gladiator school with the help of his 78 comrades. Somehow, he was going to get his freedom back.

In the year 73 BCE, Spartacus and his comrades finally made their move after carefully planning how they were going to escape. They were well-fed, fit, and well-trained fighters, but their weapons were likely kept somewhere inaccessible, probably in a separate building or well-guarded room. Spartacus, though, knew that the armory wasn't the only place where weapons were to be found. Every day, kitchen slaves brought the gladiators their meals. And there were sharp things in kitchens.

History doesn't tell us how exactly Spartacus and the others managed to get out of their shackles and cells, but they did, and they made a beeline for the kitchen. The kitchen slaves likely fled at the sight of almost 80 brawny gladiators coming at them, giving Spartacus and his men precious moments in which to grab any sharp object they could find, readying themselves for the onslaught of guards that was undoubtedly heading right for them.

It must have been a heart-pounding few minutes in that kitchen, the burly figures of the gladiators yanking open chests and upturning baskets as they hunted for anything that gleamed like metal. But those few minutes were enough. Kitchen knife in hand, Spartacus was ready when the first guard came rushing in. The guards were used to fighting in full armor for money; the gladiators knew how to fought unarmored for nothing but their lives. It was little contest. The gladiators cut down their captors with brutal efficiency and raw fear, and Spartacus led them out of the gladiator school and into the surrounding countryside.

Wounded, breathless, and fully aware that hundreds of Roman soldiers would descend upon them as soon as Batiatus sounded the alarm, Spartacus and his comrades knew that their escape wasn't finished when they stepped out of the gladiator school. Seventy-eight half-dressed, muscular slaves, many of whose faces were easily recognizable from their frequent public appearances, and all wielding some kind of a weapon, could hardly have been more conspicuous if they'd tried. They had to flee somewhere inhospitable, somewhere sparsely populated except perhaps by fellow slaves, and somewhere close enough that they could make it. Spartacus had chosen just the right spot for that purpose.

In 73 BCE, almost 2,100 years ago today, the town of Capua lay at the very feet of a majestic mountain that towered its green and rocky head thousands of feet above the surrounding farmland. Its silent peak was still and beautiful, and it was almost totally void of buildings or people. The climb wouldn't be easy, but Spartacus knew his fit gladiators could do it, and so, they headed for the flanks of the mountain as quickly as they could. Little did they know that a century after they scaled its height, the mountain would erupt in a shower of ash and lava that would bury multiple towns and kill thousands of people. Their new hiding place was none other than Mount Vesuvius.

Spartacus and his comrades may not have known that they were climbing to the peak of an active volcano, but even if they did, perhaps they would have counted it less of a risk than staying in that awful gladiator school where they all had been slowly losing their minds.

One can imagine the thrill that Spartacus felt as he and his gladiators bolted toward the towering peak. Fear nipped at his heels, driving him faster as the threat of pursuing guards chased him on, but there was something else that was exhilarating, too—something as pure and wild as the mountain wind that filled his lungs. It was freedom. He knew then, whether he lived or died or made it to the peak or not, that he would be doing it as a free man.

But he didn't die on the flank of that volcano. Instead, Spartacus, Crixus, Oenomaus, and their comrades (it is uncertain how many of the original 78 survived the flight from Capua) made it. Despite a brief battle with the pursuing guards, they made it all the way up to the sheltering peak of Mount Vesuvius, where Batiatus and his guards would have difficulty tracking them. In fact, for a moment, it felt as though they had made it to safety, but Spartacus knew better than to let his guard down.

Their escape had only just begun. Spartacus knew that the Romans would be coming, and the same law that had been true in the arena would be true now.

"Fight or die."

Chapter 5 – Ambush

With the trek to Mount Vesuvius improbably, and yet undeniably, having succeeded, Spartacus and his comrades dug in and started to prepare for the future. Whether they'd expected to get this far or not, they were quickly able to formulate a plan.

While the idea of slaves escaping and rebelling against their erstwhile masters may be heady stuff in a world where slavery has largely been abolished, there's nothing to indicate that abolition was ever on Spartacus' radar. His goal was much simpler. All he wanted to do was escape. But considering that he came from the center of the world's greatest empire at the time, escape was not a simple thing. He would have to cover thousands of miles, miles that were swarming with Roman soldiers, in order to get away from Roman captivity once and for all. And all of his comrades were coming with him.

By the time they had reached Mount Vesuvius, Spartacus, Crixus, and Oenomaus had seen to it that they would be relatively well provided for. The journey from Capua to the mountain had taken them through fertile farmland, and the men and women that were tending those fields were sitting ducks to a group of gladiators. Spartacus led his band of liberated warriors to raid the farms for food, equipment, and weapons. The success of their raids was variable when it came to much-needed equipment, but at least they could get enough food to sustain themselves for a while, as well as arm themselves more thoroughly. Exchanging kitchen knives for axes, picks, and hoes, Spartacus and his men made it to Vesuvius feeling considerably more confident than when they'd fled the gladiator school.

Finding a hiding place on Mount Vesuvius was hardly difficult. Now a barren wasteland surrounding a smoking crater, Vesuvius was once a green and fertile place, covered with foliage and vines. It was difficult to traverse, too; three sides of the mountain were rocky cliffs that dropped off hundreds of feet to certain death. There was only one way up, and Spartacus' men, once they reached the peak, carefully watched it. The gladiators holed up in the thick cover, and after some time, they realized that no one had found them. A collective sigh of relief ran through the hasty camp, and the escapees began to ask themselves a new question: now what?

The person with the answer to that question seemed to be Spartacus. He had plenty of military experience under his belt, and besides, there was something about the fire in him that lit a spark in the others. They elected him as their leader, and Crixus and Oenomaus were both seconds-in-command. There may also have been lesser-ranking commanders in the group.

Oenomaus and Crixus were both powerful gladiators in their own right, but no one could match Crixus for sheer pig-headed determination. The curly-headed gladiator had endured much in his life, and there was a bitterness in his heart that longed for more than escape. He wanted vengeance. In those early days, Spartacus managed to convince Crixus that escape was their primary goal, but there was a tension already present between the Thracian and the Gaul. The cheers of the Roman public had gone to Crixus' head. He held onto his pride to ward off his fear, forgetting that the very same people who cheered for his victory would have cheered equally for his grisly demise and defeat.

It wasn't long after the gladiator leaders had been elected that their leadership was put to the test. Bitterly complaining about the loss of his valuable gladiators, Batiatus had reported the incident to Rome, demanding that a legion come and recapture his warlike prisoners since it was certainly too great a task for him and his guards. Rome's response was not what Batiatus had hoped. And part of this was because the Roman legions were not near Rome.

The First Mithridatic War, which had kept Sulla so busy in Pontus, eventually erupted into two more wars. The Third Mithridatic War, which started in 75 BCE and wouldn't end until 63 BCE, was a large enough threat that many of the Roman legions were occupied with fighting in it. And in Spain, Quintus Sertorius, a former Marian commander, had stirred up a revolt that was almost on the same scale as Sulla's civil wars. The Roman Republic was in its death throes, and its greatness would only be reborn as the Roman Empire in several decades' time. For now, though, its legions were much too busy trying to uphold its crumbling borders to deal with a bunch of escapees.

Something did have to be done, however, and that was where Gaius Claudius Glaber came in. Glaber was a praetor, which was a high-ranking Roman official. He was told to sort out the gladiator problem so that Rome's higher ranks could continue to focus on more important matters.

Little is known about Glaber except for his involvement with fighting Spartacus. However, from his actions at Vesuvius, one can venture to deduce that his laziness was matched only by his arrogance.

In the absence of the rigorously trained legionaries, Glaber had to seek manpower elsewhere, and so, he raised an ad hoc militia on the spur of the moment. His men were recruited from the surrounding area and were largely untrained; given some armor, weapons, and pay, they were told all they had to do was capture a handful of escaped slaves. Easy, right? Recruitment wasn't hard, and Glaber didn't anticipate any part of his task as being hard at all. He believed that a bunch of dumb slaves couldn't possibly hope to stand against a Roman militia, even if it didn't consist of legionaries.

There were several factors that Glaber hadn't considered, however. The first was that Spartacus' group no longer consisted of just 78 gladiators. The landscape through which the gladiators had fled, the farms they had raided, and even the fertile flanks of the mountain were all thickly populated with slaves. Herdsmen tending their master's flocks, hapless workers tilling in the fields, even girls working in the homes of farmers—these men and women didn't swing swords or train hard as the gladiators had. In fact, they couldn't have looked more different from the muscular gladiators if they'd tried. But gladiator or no, all these Roman slaves shared one thing in common: they wanted to be free. And Spartacus, somehow, had done it. He'd broken his shackles and fled to the mountainside, and the slaves of the surrounding area followed him in droves.

By the time Glaber sought to attack and recapture Spartacus and his men, the Thracian's group numbered in the thousands, although the exact number is unknown. Glaber's 3,000 men, which was thought to be overly sufficient faced with less than a hundred escapees, would not be as adequate as he had originally thought.

The other factor Glaber hadn't thought of was that Spartacus and many of his comrades were far more than ordinary slaves. They were gladiators, and some of them saw actual battle more frequently than a Roman legionary. These men fought for their lives day in and day out, and it was all they trained for. It was all they *were*, in the eyes of their masters. What was more, Spartacus had been a Roman soldier long before he became a gladiator, and he understood how Romans commanded their troops. He knew his enemy with a bitter intimacy.

Totally failing to account for Spartacus' prowess, Glaber gathered up his band of impromptu soldiers and marched on Vesuvius. Looking at the mountain, he decided that capturing the slaves would be childishly simple. Vesuvius provided plenty of cover, but there was little in the way of provisions to be scavenged from it. Cut them off from the farmlands, Glaber reasoned, and they'd have no choice but to come down. He wouldn't even have to fight them. Starvation would be his only weapon: they would either come down from the mountain or starve up there, and either way worked for him.

Besieging Mount Vesuvius wouldn't be difficult, either, with its single route up and down from the peak. Glaber brought his army over to the only way up the mountain and plopped them down for a leisurely siege that shouldn't make anyone break a sweat. In fact, he seems to have failed to send scouts out or even arrange sentries among his ranks. They just kicked back their heels and relaxed, waiting for a few half-starved and desperate slaves to come stumbling out of the bushes toward them.

They didn't expect a group of warriors to appear out of the cliffs themselves and attack.

Spartacus knew that, large though his force may now be, attacking the Romans head-on would be a death sentence. Instead, he decided to do what Roman commanders often failed to account for—he thought outside the box. Glaber would be expecting Spartacus and his men to come straight down the mountain toward them on the one route that could be taken on foot. So, Spartacus' men would do the opposite.

They would come down the cliffs.

The men and women in the camp set to work. Gathering some of the many green vines that grew all over the mountain, they braided them together, forming springy green ropes that could hold the weight of a powerful gladiator. Once the ropes were done and night had fallen, Spartacus and the bravest of his men headed for the clifftops.

Quietly, they secured the ropes at the top of the cliffs, gripped their weapons, and rappelled down the steep and rocky slopes to land feet first in the middle of the Roman camp.

Utter chaos broke loose. Torches were knocked over, and screams echoed through the night, as sleeping soldiers found themselves faced with desperate bare-chested gladiators wielding biting axes and razor-sharp cleavers. Terror reigned in the camp as the disorganized militia abruptly decided that no matter how much Glaber was paying them, it wasn't enough to fight these men who'd appeared from nowhere. They scattered, being cut down where they fled. Glaber is not mentioned in any historical account following the Battle of Mount Vesuvius, and while he may simply have retired and faded into obscurity after this embarrassment, it's entirely possible that he was one of the many who fell that day in the face of the gladiators.

The Romans were utterly routed. They fled back down the mountain, abandoning their camp just as it was. To Spartacus and his followers, the emptied camp was a boon, giving them an abundance of armor, weapons, and horses. They were able to hold real weapons again at last. There was also the presence of something that many of the slaves hadn't possessed in a long time, if they'd ever even had it before: money. To people whose right to own anything had long since been ripped away, the sight of gold and silver coins must have been quite intoxicating. Spartacus made himself even more popular when he decided that the entire bounty of their spoils would be fairly and equally divided among all the slaves, even though he could have easily kept it all for himself.

One can only imagine the scale of the jubilation in that destroyed Roman camp that night. Perhaps they found some wine among the Roman belongings. Maybe there was dancing, and perhaps even a little music, knowing that they had just accomplished the impossible. They had money and security now. They had a leader they trusted.

But that leader, as he gathered together the weapons and armor, knew that their fight was far from over. Their initial escape may have ended, but the war was just beginning.

The Third Servile War was born beneath the cliffs that night. And the scale of its devastation and destruction had never been seen in a slave uprising before.

Chapter 6 – Facing the Legions

Illustration II: A map of events according to Plutarch

Glaber's defeat by Spartacus and the rest of the slaves did not strike the Romans as a threat. Instead, it was something potentially even worse to a culture that prided itself on being superior on every level, including the divine one: it was an insult. A hideous insult to the

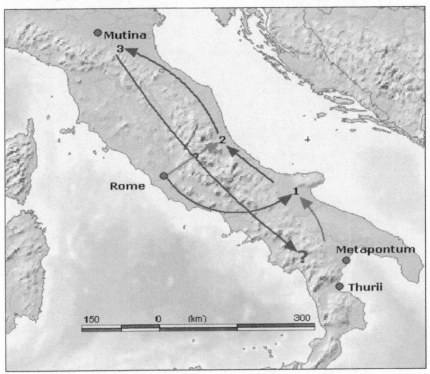

1 - Gellius' defeats Crixus
2 - Spartacus defeats Lentulus
3 - Spartacus defeats Cassius

Crixus' followers
Spartacus'' followers
Gellius' Legion
Lentulus' Legion

prowess of Rome. The fact that a bunch of lowly slaves was able to best a praetor was as good as if Spartacus himself had walked up to a consul and spat in his eye.

Rome was determined to sweep Spartacus and the defeat of Glaber under the rug as quickly as possible. Even though the legions were otherwise occupied, the leadership of Rome decided that the best way to get rid of this pesky band of escaped slaves would be to send a couple of the legions to wipe them out once and for all. Another praetor was elected for the role of defeating Spartacus: Publius Varinius.

Varinius was a more cautious man than Glaber. Given the command of several thousand legionaries—likely around 6,000—he decided that facing Spartacus would take some real thinking, not simply barging around as Glaber had done. He was also aware that Spartacus' ranks had swollen vastly from the 78 men who'd escaped Capua, as there had been several thousand at the Battle of Mount Vesuvius. Varinius could never have anticipated exactly how many slaves had joined Spartacus' movement, however. The truth was that there were already about 40,000 men fighting on Spartacus' side.

One move of Spartacus', however, was working to Varinius' advantage. Growing in numbers, the slaves were getting bolder. They were also running out of provisions. Mount Vesuvius had been a good hiding place for a hundred men; forty thousand men were beginning to stretch its resources very thin. Spartacus was being forced to send raiding parties farther and farther afield in a bid to feed his growing army.

Varinius knew that it wouldn't be necessary for him to scale Vesuvius. He could attack Spartacus out in the open country now, and that was exactly what he intended to do. Dividing the bulk of his army up into two groups, he sent them out in a pincer attack, attempting to crush Spartacus' army between the long arms of his own. The first group, commanded by Lucius Furius, consisted of

2,000 men. The rest of the army was split between Lucius Cossinius and a small vanguard with Varinius.

Furius and his men reached the slaves first, unfortunately for them. A group of slaves, possibly commanded by Crixus, lay in wait for the Romans and launched a devastating surprise attack. Furius' column was utterly destroyed, his men routed, and the commander himself killed in the battle. Spartacus himself had gone hunting for Cossinius; the Roman commander may not have expected the slaves to actively seek him out, but they did. Around six miles from Vesuvius, Spartacus found Cossinius preparing for a battle at Herculaneum. He attacked, decimated Cossinius' legions, and set Cossinius himself to flight. Spartacus turned to search for Varinius next, but some of the slaves broke off from the main army and pursued Cossinius as he fled. They caught up to him in the end and butchered him, just like thousands of them had been butchered for the entertainment of his people.

The remnants of the Roman legions regrouped with Varinius, tattered, shocked, and battle-weary from fighting the slaves. As for Spartacus, he realized now that he didn't need Vesuvius anymore. He'd just beaten the Roman legions themselves in open battle, and his own forces were tremendously large, larger than the legions could hope to send against him thanks to their involvement in distant wars. Spartacus realized that he could go wherever he wanted. And where he wanted to be was as far as possible from Rome.

He swung his slaves to the south, hoping to find a route to freedom, and marched away from the home of their oppressors. Crixus was dismayed. The brotherly affection between him and Spartacus erupted, as it often did, into heavy arguing. Victory against the legions had gone to Crixus' head; he believed that they could achieve more. That they could damage Rome as sorely as it had damaged them, and that they could take from Rome what it loved as surely as it had taken away their freedom. Anger and bitterness had been building for so long in Crixus' heart, fueled by every fight in the gladiatorial arena, that he wanted nothing more than to satiate his lust for vengeance. But Spartacus held firm. He wanted to set these people free, not lead them into battle. So, they journeyed south, and Varinius, replenishing his numbers, followed warily behind.

The Roman finally was able to pitch his battle against Spartacus when they'd reached the distant southern town of Lucania. Here, Varinius ran into trouble before he even saw Spartacus and the slaves. Winter was approaching, and the morale among his troops was at a desperate low as they faced the dropping temperatures. What was more, rumors had been circulating through the camp that Spartacus was dividing the spoils equally among his men. Varinius certainly didn't do the same, and some of the lower-ranking soldiers were beginning to wonder if they were fighting on the right side of this war. By now, Spartacus' army did not consist solely of escaped slaves. There were freedmen there now, fighting for a better life, as they knew that the Roman Republic was crumbling around them and hoped that Spartacus would be able to lead them to something better. None of Spartacus' men were slaves anymore: they were rebels.

As a result, Varinius' men began to refuse to fight at all. While he could punish them harshly for desertion and for disobeying his orders, Varinius couldn't physically force them to fight, and so it was with a reduced army and rock-bottom morale that the praetor turned to meet Spartacus at Lucania.

Varinius came perilously close to sharing the fate of his commanders. His unhappy troops clashed miserably with Spartacus' fired-up warriors in a battle that rapidly turned into a humiliating rout. Despite Varinius' more careful tactics, his men were put to flight as surely as Glaber's had been. In fact, the praetor himself was almost captured and/or killed. Rebels seized him, pulling him from his horse. Somehow—likely thanks to a rally of his troops—Varinius was saved, but the rebels returned triumphantly to their camp, leading the praetor's horse between them. The majestic animal was a symbol to them of how close they'd come to taking down a praetor when, only months before, their backs had been covered in scars from the lashes of mere farmers and miners.

Having defeated every adversary that had been set before him, Spartacus entered the winter of 73 BCE feeling confident that he would finally be able to achieve what classical historians presume was his end goal: going home. His army was tens of thousands strong, and it would continue to grow to a force that eventually numbered as many as 120,000. Crixus was urging him to march on Rome itself, to take down the city and rebuild a better world. Dizzy with the scent of victory, many of Spartacus' men would have followed him if he had chosen to lay siege to the capital of the world. But Spartacus had tasted victory many times before—serving in the legions, fighting in the gladiatorial arena, and now as a rebel leader. Victory was good, but home was better.

Still, he was aware that moving 120,000 rebels out of the Roman Republic was no mean feat, and there would be battles to fight along the way. That winter, the Romans left Spartacus largely alone, and he and his men dug in and trained hard as the days grew shorter and the nights colder. Spartacus drove his men hard, encouraging him with his charismatic leadership, as he knew that their victories were nothing compared to what was still to come. They may have beaten some legions, but those legions hadn't been the experienced, battle-hardened men who'd just come home from Spain and Pontus. Those were war veterans fresh off the front, and this time, Spartacus knew, they wouldn't underestimate the rebels.

When spring brought its warm green blush to the Italian countryside, the rift between Spartacus and Crixus grew even wider. Spartacus wanted to take the army straight toward Gaul, seeking the easiest and quickest route out of Roman territory. He wanted to go home, and he wanted to send the slaves home, or at least into freedom. But Crixus had been living off the spoils of his raiding and plundering for too long. He liked fighting. He liked winning more than just the cheers of a jabbering crowd. He liked his growing wealth. And perhaps he believed that the rebels could overthrow Rome itself.

Spartacus and Crixus could not agree, but Spartacus wouldn't force his friend—a man who had become like a brother to him, if a somewhat quarrelsome one—to obey him. Besides, many of the rebels wanted to follow Crixus and continue the war. So, Spartacus split the army in two. He and those who wanted to escape the Roman Republic turned toward Gaul; Crixus and his fellow raiders, numbering around 30,000, went south, heading deep into Italy where the farmlands were waiting to be plundered.

It was a terrible mistake.

Rome had finally awoken to the real danger posed by the rebels. Clearly, this was a problem beyond the praetors; it would take real legions, battle-seasoned and commanded by men of the highest rank, to put a stop to the chaos that Spartacus and Crixus were sowing all over the Republic. Multiple Roman legions were sent out, and these were commanded by the consuls. One was Gnaeus Cornelius Lentulus Clodianus, and the other was Lucius Gellius Publicola.

Publicola struck first. Discovering Crixus' smaller force under the shadows of Mount Gargano, where they were raiding Roman towns with merry abandon, the consul decided that it was time to teach these arrogant rebels a lesson. He attacked.

Crixus may have done well to flee, to find a defensible position, or to seek reinforcements from Spartacus. Yet at his heart, Crixus was a gladiator, not a commander. He only knew one way to respond to a threat: to attack. Seeing the legions rush down upon him, Crixus knew no fear. He ordered his men forward, and he rushed into the battle with the kind of courage that had kept him alive in the arena.

It did not serve him so well here, not when there were tens of thousands of soldiers involved, and not when he should have been working on strategies instead of charging blindly into battle. Thirty thousand rebels started the battle with Publicola on that bloody day in the spring of 72 BCE; only ten thousand were left when the fight was over. And Crixus was not one of them. It was a hopeless, humiliating defeat, and it was the last battle Crixus would ever fight.

When the news reached Spartacus, it broke his heart. As much as Crixus had argued with him, as warlike and arrogant as the Gaul had been, they had been friends in the worst of circumstances. The darkness and the chains back in Capua had bonded them as brothers. And now dear, stupid, proud, stubborn, brave Crixus was dead.

Spartacus' grief turned dark and bitter in his heart. He remembered the glorious funerals that the Romans had always held to honor the dead; he remembered, also, having to fight to commemorate dead Romans. He remembered the roots of the gladiatorial games, and a dark idea formed in his mind. Something about the death of Crixus snapped something deep inside Spartacus. He wanted to do to the Romans what they had done to him, to Crixus, and to the others.

It is presumed that the body of the dead rebel general was never recovered, but Spartacus was determined to give him a funeral anyway, a funeral worthy of a general and not a mere gladiator. Gladiators died in the public eye and were buried in ignominy, but Crixus was going to be given the send-off of a high-ranking Roman official. And that meant that Spartacus would need to throw gladiatorial games of his own to honor the dead.

It was a bitterly twisted day when the black smoke of Crixus' empty pyre rose up against the Italian sun and Spartacus watched as his gladiators lined up to face each other. Only these gladiators weren't slaves and foreigners. They were prisoners of war. They were Romans. Spartacus watched with satisfaction as he saw these well-trained warriors forget their honor, their glory, and their social standing. He watched the look in their eyes change from triumph to fear. He watched them fight the way he had once fought: desperately, in terror, for their lives.

Fight or die.

Chapter 7 – The Lone Volunteer

When the Roman prisoners all lay dead around the camp, and Spartacus was satisfied that Crixus had been thoroughly honored, he turned his attention to vengeance. The army that had killed his friend and destroyed a large portion of his army was still out there, and they were rapidly maneuvering to do to Spartacus what they had done to Crixus. Clodianus was heading as fast as his men could march for the Alps, hoping to corner Spartacus before he could escape the Republic, while Publicola was stalking him from behind. Their hope was to crush Spartacus and the rebels between the two of them and put a stop to the rebellion once and for all. They were expecting Spartacus to keep fleeing toward the Alps, toward home.

Home was where Spartacus was going, but he was by no means going to flee the consuls. He was ready to attack now. Even though the legions were better armed than his rebels, Spartacus had an ace up his sleeve: a strong cavalry regiment. They had been unable to procure horses when they had first escaped from Capua, but Spartacus and many of the rebels were Thracian, and they'd been taming the wild horses that roamed the mountainsides of Thrace for generations. Capturing wild horses or stealing farm horses and turning them into reliable cavalry mounts was child's play for these men.

One would like to imagine that Spartacus had kept Varinius' horse for himself, a strong, beautiful animal that had once borne a Roman praetor and now carried the gladiator who had defeated him. Either way, Spartacus had a cavalry, and he put it to good use. Clodianus was still waiting for the approach of a lumbering band of infantry when Spartacus and his cavalry burst out of the landscape and swooped down upon the legions. Caught by surprise, Clodianus and his men didn't have the time to rally. Spartacus' cavalry cut straight through Clodianus' legions, and the consul was sent back to Rome with his tail between his legs, his army routed, and all of his supplies stolen by the rebels.

Punching right through the consuls' trap, Spartacus continued toward the Alps as the winter of 72 BCE settled cold and dark on the landscape. Clodianus and Publicola, thoroughly beaten, had to return to Rome in ignominy. The leaders of Rome—the two single men wielding the most power in the whole Roman Republic—had let it down. The rebels were still on the loose, and their force was still growing. The Senate, however, decided that its consuls were clearly unfit to lead the army. They perhaps also thought that the risk of both of them getting killed in a battle would cause too much instability and panic in Rome; already, the Romans were terrified that Spartacus was going to wheel around and attack the great city itself.

Another leader would have to be found, one who would willingly face the rebels and seek a resounding and lasting victory. The Senate began to ask for volunteers among the patriarchy. Most men backed away, knowing that being beaten by the rebels was political suicide.

Most men. One—and one alone—volunteered to go and meet Spartacus on the battlefield. And that man was Marcus Licinius Crassus.

Crassus had been rolling in money for years. His wily real estate schemes and smooth-talking politics had won him both wealth and power, and his reputation for being a generous host had also gifted him with popularity. That Spanish cave overlooking the sea must have seemed like it was ages ago, and yet Crassus, for all his wealth, could still not satiate a furious hunger that burned inside him. That hunger was envy, and that envy was of Pompey. The young general had amassed glory upon glory in his battles in the Mithridatic Wars, Sulla's civil wars, and now in the Sertorian War in Spain. Sulla had even bestowed upon Pompey the highest possible honor for a military man: a triumph, or a long, glamorous parade through the streets of Rome. Crassus wanted a triumph, too. He wanted to be as glorious in the eyes of the people as Pompey. He wanted to play second fiddle to no one.

To Crassus' delight, Pompey was thoroughly out of the way when the call came for volunteers to go up against Spartacus. Sertorius' revolt in Spain was still in full force, and so, Pompey's hands were full with fighting in the land where Crassus had once hidden in a dark cave. This was Crassus' chance to shine. He jumped at the opportunity, and since he was the only man who volunteered to fight Spartacus, he was immediately given the job and the full command of the legions in Italy.

Morale among those legions had been low throughout the rebellion, and they had never been lower than they were at that moment. Many remembered how others had refused to fight Spartacus at all back when they were under Varinius' command; perhaps those who refused had chosen wisely, considering the utter defeat that the legions had suffered at Lucania. Others had tasted briefly of victory against Crixus only to see Spartacus slip out of their fingers once again. Perhaps they were tired of the surprises that Spartacus was continually throwing at them—abseiling down cliff walls on vines or mustering a whole cavalry regiment out of nowhere. They never knew what this Thracian was going to do next.

Another factor that must have had an effect on Roman morale was the fact that the war was being fought in Italy, which was the homeland of many of these legionaries. They would have seen acres of farmland, villages, and towns that looked like the places where they'd grown up. They would have also seen them all razed to the ground, trampled into blood and dirt, and raided bare. Spartacus was a hero to the rebels, but to the legions, he was a terrifying threat. What was more, he was inspiring thousands of slaves to leave their posts and follow him. The implication for the Roman economy was great, but greater still was the fear that free Romans had of their own slaves now. They were aware that there were more slaves than free people living in the Roman Republic. If all the slaves revolted, it could spell death and disaster.

Thus, it was a very disheartened army that Crassus found at his disposal, one that was sick of the humiliation of being defeated by a mere gladiator. Crassus was good with words, but it would take more than smooth-talking to inspire this disheartened bunch—and before going up against Spartacus, Crassus knew that he would have to whip this sorry band of miserable legionaries into shape. Perhaps he could have done this with inspiration or the promise of great rewards. Instead, Crassus wielded the greatest weapon of all against his own men: fear.

The word "decimation" today is defined as large-scale killing or destruction. In ancient Rome, it had a much more specific meaning, coming from the Latin root of "decem," or "ten." Yet even then, the word was ominous, and it was guaranteed to strike terror into the heart of any Roman soldier. Decimation was a thing to be horribly feared, and with good reason, as it meant the killing of one-tenth of a Roman legion as punishment for poor performance in battle.

Even in the 1st century BCE, decimation was already an ancient punishment, and it had only been rarely used even when it was fairly popular around the 5th century BCE. In fact, it hadn't been used for decades when Crassus strutted into his command of the legions, but that didn't stop him from inflicting it upon his men. As soon as the announcement was made, a hush of silent terror fell upon the Roman camp. Every soldier knew that he might not see the end of the day.

One by one, lots were cast for each of the legions that Crassus wanted to punish for their inability to stop Spartacus. It was a deadly gamble, a game of human lives. Out of every ten soldiers, one would have to die. And once that man was chosen, the nine comrades who lived were forced to take up heavy cudgels and bludgeon their brother-in-arms to death. These men had fought together, lived together, and were ready to die together on the battlefield. Instead, they had to kill each other, brutally and violently, bones crunching under the savage blows of the clubs, and the blood of friends splattering hot and salty on their faces.

When it was done, Crassus' army was one-tenth smaller than it had been before his decimation. The men who remained were given only raw barley to eat that night, and they ate it slowly, their fear making the bitter grain turn to sawdust on their tongues. They knew one thing for sure: angering Crassus would be a terrible mistake.

There was no adversary that could frighten them as much as Crassus just did. And so, these men would fight to the death for him, their lives suddenly governed by the same rule that had driven Spartacus from one victory to the next in the gladiatorial games. Now, fight or die had become the reality for Romans who considered themselves to be free.

Chapter 8 – At the Feet of the Alps

Illustration III: It's easy to see why the Italian Alps appeared so forbidding to Spartacus' men

The terrified troops that now found themselves under the command

of Crassus might have expected to be marched immediately to the north. But Crassus, heartless though he may have been, was also a wily commander. He knew that simply punishing his men and sending them back into battle wasn't going to be an effective strategy. Instead, he began to train them, working through the winter by taking money out of his own pocket to equip and train the eight legions he'd been given, which was around 40,000 men, to the best of his ability. This was not simply about winning a war or defending his country from a rebellion. To Crassus, this was personal. It didn't even matter that Crassus had never laid eyes on Spartacus before— the Thracian now represented to Crassus the only obstacle lying between him and equal greatness to Pompey. Envy proved to be a powerful motivator.

Meanwhile, Spartacus continued to push north as fast as his men could march, but there was one more mighty obstacle lying between them and the Alps: Mutina, which was commanded by Gaius Cassius Longinus Varus. Now called Modena, this city was where Longinus ruled over Cisalpine Gaul as its governor, and it was the last great obstacle between Spartacus and the Alps. The gladiator general knew that if he could reach the Alps and cross them, he'd be almost home free. No Roman legion would pursue him over those great mountains.

But Spartacus also had to hurry. Winter was coming; 72 BCE was drawing to a close, and he needed to get his men over those mountains before the snow made them utterly impassable. If that took him through Mutina, then so be it, no matter who was standing in his way.

Longinus' son, who shared the same name as his father but is better known as Cassius, would later become legendary for his involvement in the assassination of Julius Caesar. But all that was almost thirty years in the future, and right now, Longinus was just a governor bent on protecting his piece of the Roman Republic from the marauding army of the gladiators—and they were indeed marauding. Spartacus now had more than 100,000 followers, and all those men and women had to be fed somehow. They had been plundering ever since they left Capua, and those raids were now occurring on a grand scale. While the defeat of the legions had left them with plenty of armor and weapons, provisions still needed to be scrounged from the farmlands. The slaves that continued to escape and join the rebellion had little regard for the lives of those who had oppressed them. Civilians were killed, crops destroyed, and livestock was slaughtered and carried off to feed the insatiable army.

The raiding was made worse by the fact that Spartacus was pushing as fast as he could, refusing to stop or slow down for anything, not even to carry provisions with him. He slaughtered the pack animals for food and burned all the supplies that couldn't be easily carried. Ruthlessly pushing his army—which by now included children and the elderly, as slaves brought their families with them, hoping to take them to freedom—Spartacus reached Mutina before winter came.

Here, once again, a Roman army stood between him and his homeland, and once again, Spartacus and his men rallied to defeat it. Longinus didn't stand a chance. The provincial army was thoroughly defeated at Mutina, and the way was thrown wide open for Spartacus to take his gigantic army to the Alps and cross over into Thrace.

Spartacus was almost home. But he didn't go. Instead, his entire enormous contingent, exhausted from weeks of hard marching, came shuddering to a halt at the feet of the mighty Alps.

With the nip of winter in the air, the plain where Spartacus made his camp was richly painted in reds and browns, the glowing colors of fall still all around them. It looked warm and inviting; the crops were still ripe in the fields that his people were plundering. There were cooking fires and the smell of wood smoke and children laughing down here on the plain. But ahead of them, the Alps rose like a tremendous rampart, a monumental rock wall stabbing up into the sky, already streaked with snow. There were no gentle rises, no apparent pass, and no visible way to cross those great mountains. Spartacus knew it could be done, but it didn't look that way. The mountains were more than daunting. They looked impassable.

He hadn't come all this way just to give up because of the mountains he'd always known he had to climb, though. It had seemed an easier task when there had just been 78 strong and fit gladiators to get to the other side. Even with tens of thousands of followers, Spartacus seemed to have wanted to try. But something stopped him on that plain in the fall of 72 BCE, at the very feet of the last obstacle standing between him and the homeland he was yearning for. No one really knows why. It's possible that his vast following was simply too daunted by the great peaks. Perhaps, news of Thrace had reached them, too. All was not well in the homeland that Spartacus wanted to return to.

Even though Thrace had, for many years, been more or less under Roman control, it was not a province of the Roman Republic, not when Spartacus had walked those heady mountainsides, anyway. It was a client kingdom: meekly submissive to Rome and obliged to provide the great Republic with some of its resources but still able to govern itself as it pleased. Except the winds of change were blowing across Spartacus' ancestral highlands, and they didn't smell good. Rumors were reaching him that Rome had actually appointed the new king. That made Thrace little more than a Roman province— and it meant that the Thracian king was a Roman ally. How could Spartacus return to a country governed by his enemies? If Rome found out that Spartacus and the other escaped slaves were in Thrace, the new king would easily hand them over. And then it would have been better if they'd simply stayed put and remained slaves for the rest of their lives.

To make matters worse, Crixus' ambitions had infected many of the rebels. Defeating a Roman consul, then a governor, — was a mighty and incredible feat, and it went to their heads. Spartacus' tantalizing offer of returning back home had lost its savor in the face of victory upon victory. What was home in comparison with continuing to plunder these rich fields? There were whispers among the rebels of marching on Rome itself, taking down the city, and building something better. The sweet sound of liberty had been drowned out in the crescendo of power.

We can only speculate on which of these factors—or, perhaps, which combination of these factors—caused Spartacus to do what he did next. Almost within sight of Thrace, the Thracian turned around. He headed back down from the Alps and began to move toward the south of Italy, his men free once more to plunder as they pleased. Not all of them chose to continue raiding Italy, however. Spartacus allowed his followers to choose whether they wanted to risk crossing the frigid Alps for the promise of going home or to stay with the main army and attempt to conquer more of the Roman Republic. Ten thousand men wisely chose to go back to their homelands. As Plutarch did, we could assume that Spartacus' heart went with them, but he felt a duty to remain as the military leader of the men who refused to cross the Alps.

For a time, the fortune and skill that had so favored Spartacus since his rebellion began continued to pursue them as they moved toward the southernmost tip of Italy. Crassus was training his troops, biding his time, and so, Spartacus was largely unopposed except by local garrisons as he and his men swept ever southward. They moved fast, too; fast enough that many in Rome were terrified that the time had come at last that their slaves would overthrow them. Spartacus knew better than to attempt to attack the great city itself, however. This may have been the plan eventually, but he had to build up their strength, equipment, and numbers first. Instead, he kept going past Rome and pushed toward the sea.

Sometime in the winter of 72/71 BCE, they arrived at the southwestern tip of Italy, a province then known as Bruttium, where he and his men were using their plunder to their advantage. The supplies they didn't need were traded (many merchants didn't seem to care who they dealt with, Roman or rebel, as long as they were paid) for metals with which to manufacture more armor and weaponry. Spartacus' army was made up of ex-slaves, after all. They knew how to work with their hands.

Perhaps in preparation for fighting a bigger city, Spartacus set his sights on the town of Thurii. The ancient town, whose foundations were laid in the mid-5th century BCE, was subjected to a swift and efficient attack from Spartacus and his men. It appears as though it may have surrendered quickly and willingly; there was no damage to the city, and there does not appear to have been many casualties according to historical records, although Spartacus did compel the citizens to pay him a heavy tribute, not to mention his men who helped themselves to supplies. It was the first time that the rebels had taken a town.

It was also one of their last great victories. Crassus had patiently watched and waited as the rebels dug in and spent the winter happily in Thurii. His men had been training hard, driven by the terror of their leader. He knew that if he was going to stop Spartacus, he wouldn't have much time—at least, not if he was going to do it personally. Rumor had it that Pompey's attempts to put down the revolt in Spain were growing more and more successful. Soon, he would win, and he would come back to Rome, and he would take over from Crassus, and there would be no glory for the jealous praetor.

Envy in the north. Greed in the south. There would-be no-good end to this tale.

Chapter 9 – Defeat

When spring came again in 71 BCE, both Crassus and Spartacus were on the move.

Spartacus' goal at this point in time is uncertain, although he may well have been trying to march on Rome; his men left Thurii and headed northward, their ranks swollen with numbers, steel weapons gleaming in the hands of each rebel soldier. Three long years of war had beaten Spartacus' army from a rag-tag bunch of escaped slaves into a real military force, good enough to beat even Rome's best. Now, he moved them toward Lucania, where they had fought that glorious victory against Varinius in the very first year of the war. Perhaps the soil upon which so much Roman blood had been spilled would prove to be a good battleground once more.

Crassus' goal, on the other hand, is abundantly clear. He wanted to stop Spartacus, and he wanted to do it as quickly and gloriously as possible. As his practice of decimation had proven, Crassus wouldn't let mere ethics or moral issues stand in his way. He wanted victory, he wanted it fast, and he wanted it at all costs.

When Spartacus' army began to move, Crassus moved just as quickly. He arrayed six of his eight legions along the borders of Picenum, near Picentia, and remained in command of them. The other two legions were entrusted to Crassus' legate, a man named Mummius. Some sources say that these were the very same legions that had once been commanded by the two consuls, the legions that had let Rome down once before. And they were about to do it again.

Spartacus and his men continued to journey north, possibly to Rome or maybe back to the Alps. Perhaps Spartacus had finally managed to convince his wayward army that going home was better than any amount of glory. Or maybe he, too, now believed that Rome was theirs for the taking. Either way, they moved north, just as Crassus had anticipated. Soon, it began to appear to Spartacus that they had no choice except to keep going north. He was likely unaware of Crassus' position at Picentia, but he did know that there was a Roman army following him and that they were very close behind.

Mummius and both his legions had taken a long, circular route around Spartacus' forces. They were now shadowing Spartacus from the south, trying to pressure him into moving more and more northward and straight into the open arms of Crassus and the bulk of the Roman army. Crassus hoped that the sight of two legions— around 10,000 men—would be enough to spook Spartacus into moving faster north. He did give Mummius strict orders, however, not to engage Spartacus under any circumstances. Those same legions had suffered a humiliating defeat under greater commanders than just a legate, as two consuls together hadn't been able to make them beat Spartacus. "Not even a skirmish," Crassus had ordered Mummius sharply.

Unfortunately for Crassus, Spartacus' men knew full well that they'd already fought and beaten two Roman legions, and Mummius' men didn't exactly strike fear into their hearts. If Spartacus' men were aware that Mummius was following them, they appear to have ignored him, waiting for him to make his move.

It seems that Mummius suffered from the same disease as Crassus did: he wanted glory, and he wanted it all to himself. Unlike Crassus, though, Mummius wasn't a cool, calculated military commander who had been hardened by years of tribulation. He thought he knew best, and he also thought he could be the one to beat Spartacus at last. When the opportunity presented itself, Mummius was ready for it. It's uncertain what exactly the circumstances were surrounding the next battle of the Third Servile War; perhaps Spartacus' troops had let their guard down, perhaps they were encamped somewhere indefensible one night, or perhaps Mummius just decided that he could achieve what two consuls hadn't.

Either way, Mummius disobeyed Crassus. He attacked the rebels with his two legions, perhaps hoping for an element of surprise. Surprised though Spartacus might have been, he responded with a violence and a capability that Mummius hadn't been expecting. When the Romans charged, a wall of shining shields coming toward the rebels, the rebels did not flee. Instead, they attacked in a foaming wave of rage, led by the fearsome Spartacus. Their battle cry echoed from one hill to the other, and when they struck, they struck like a thunderbolt. The Roman line could have held, perhaps, if the legionaries had done their duty. But they remembered too well the rout of the previous year when friends and comrades had fallen and died all around them. And when the tidal wave of rebels struck against the standing rocks of the Romans, the line crumbled, not because of casualties but simply because of fear. This means the Roman legionaries did the unthinkable: they fled, throwing down their arms as they went. Even Mummius wheeled his horse around, abandoned his troops, and whipped the beast into the best gallop it could muster, carrying him as swiftly as possible away from the battle.

The fight with Mummius was less a battle than it was a total disgrace. Perhaps somewhat bemused to have so easily beaten yet another set of Roman legions, Spartacus and his men brushed him off as a distraction and kept on moving north while Mummius' legions fled in terror. Perhaps unwisely, they headed back to the main army, where Crassus was surprised to see them. He was even more surprised to see the state that the men were in. When the legionaries had left his army to shadow Spartacus, they had been well-armed. They each had carried a massive wooden shield, a dagger, a meter-long sword called a *spatha*, and a spear. Now, they returned bedraggled and empty-handed, their weapons left behind. Yet there were not many dead or wounded.

Crassus knew from just looking at them that they had seen battle and that they had fled from it. When Mummius arrived and confirmed what Crassus already suspected, he was utterly incensed. Mummius had directly disobeyed Crassus' orders, and the result was a massive drop in morale and the loss of many expensive weapons. Crassus had furnished the army with those weapons out of his own pocket—and what was more, the show of cowardice angered him. Dropping one's weapons in flight was considered to be the height of disgrace all over the ancient world. Crassus wanted this war to glorify him, to make him wonderful, a second Pompey, Crassus Magnus perhaps. Instead, his men had run from the battlefield, and they'd made a fool out of him.

Crassus did not take well to being made a fool of, and he responded with bitter retaliation. Mummius was harshly punished—it is not specified what exactly was done to him, but Crassus may well have punished him physically—and, according to some accounts, this was when the decimation of the two legions took place. Whatever else Crassus did to punish the cowardly legions, he established himself once more in the minds of his army as being far more terrifying than Spartacus. After that, no more legionaries ran away from battle.

The damage, however, was done. Spartacus knew that there were Romans in the area, and he tried to act with more caution. What happened next is a little hazy in the historical accounts. According to Plutarch, he somehow discovered Crassus' army at Picentia without actually engaging them, perhaps by the use of scouts, and then turned back toward Bruttium, knowing that he couldn't beat Crassus. It seems unlikely, however, given that the last time two Roman legions had tried to trap Spartacus between them, he'd simply punched through them and continued on his way.

Appian's account gives a more likely explanation for Spartacus' return toward Bruttium. Spartacus, having encountered the Romans, became cautious. He started to doubt their plan of marching on Rome (if that was the plan at all), advocating instead to move straight back to the Alps and cross over them as they should have done the previous fall. Once again, a group of men refused to listen to him. About 10,000 rebels split off from the main army, following an unnamed leader. It was the last time Spartacus would see them alive.

This new little rebel faction moved closer to Crassus' army, encamping themselves somewhere near him. They did not last long. Crassus discovered them and struck, heavily and savagely, his men driven on with the knowledge that dying in battle was a better alternative to being bludgeoned to death by their own comrades. Several thousand rebels perished, and 900 were taken prisoner. The rest were scattered, their hopes of glory torn apart and thrown to the winds. Some made it back to Spartacus to warn him, but it was already too late. Crassus was coming.

Crassus' troops were now more ready than ever to fight the rebels. They'd had their first taste of victory since the death of Crixus, and they were hungry for more, ready to prove to the Roman Republic that they were still worthy of the title of being the greatest army in the world. None of Spartacus' wily tricks were going to work this time; pitched battle, the type that he had been trying to avoid ever since escaping from Capua, was inevitable. Spartacus would have to fight the Roman legions in the open for the first time, and he knew it could be disastrous.

If he had known just how disastrous it would be, Spartacus might never have even tried to stand against Crassus. The Romans he'd dealt with before had been cowards—Batiatus with his red-hot iron, Varinius abandoning his horse to flee, even Publicola and Clodianus with their inability to get their legions to defeat him. But Crassus was driven by a loathing that devoured any form of fear, and his men fought with the same kind of crazy desperation that Spartacus had known in the gladiatorial arena. When he fought them, he saw something familiar in their eyes—terror. And this time, it wasn't Spartacus that they were afraid of. They fought the way he'd fought other gladiators and wild animals—not because they wanted to fight him but because their own version of Batiatus was waiting for them if they failed to fight well. For the Roman legions, life had been reduced to one brutal fact: fight or die.

The motivator of fear proved to be just as powerful for the legionaries as it had been for the gladiators. Spartacus' rebels were unprepared for the full force of legionaries fighting their hearts out. When they clashed, which probably took place a few weeks after the battle with Mummius, the battle was a disaster, and for the first time, Spartacus himself was forced to retreat. Seeing that the battle was about to turn from mere defeat into annihilation, he took what was left of his men and fled, leaving 6,000 rebels dead on the field.

Spartacus and his men limped back toward Bruttium, shaken by their awful defeat and by the new zest for battle they'd seen in the Romans. For the first time since their revolt, the Romans had fought with a fire that could match that of the slaves. It was the beginning of the end for Spartacus, and he knew it. The fearless faith that his men had had in him was shaken now by defeat, and to make matters worse, Spartacus didn't know how to inspire them anymore. He had been promising them that they could go home. Now, though, their lust for victory had dragged them back into Italy when they had stood on the very threshold of freedom.

Spartacus' terrible suspicions were coming true. He wasn't going to be able to save them; they should have crossed the Alps when they had reached them in the first place. Now, they were all the way across the country from the Alps, with nowhere to flee except the ocean. Flee they did, however, heading deeper and deeper into the "toe" of Italy, having nowhere else to go. Crassus was hounding them now, engaging them in countless little skirmishes, each one more costly than the last. The rebels began to perish, the army fragmenting, and Spartacus was finally losing control over his massive force. It seemed as though the end was near, as if there was nothing more that Spartacus could do.

But just as Spartacus didn't give up back in the dark cells of Capua, he didn't give up now. Like he had done on the peak of Mount Vesuvius, Spartacus came up with a plan—and this one would be the most unorthodox of them all.

Chapter 10 – Betrayed by the Pirates

The Mediterranean might be the playground of tourists today, but thousands of years ago, it was ruled by pirates.

As early as 1300 BCE, Egyptian pharaohs were writing letters to Far Eastern rulers, telling them about their pirate problem, a problem that was plundering and raiding their shores. This was done by a group known as the Lukka, native to modern-day Turkey. A few hundred years later, in the time of Ramesses the Great (the pharaoh popularly considered to star in the biblical book of Exodus), the fearsome Sea Peoples ravaged the countries along the shore of the Mediterranean, destroying entire cities. Ramesses was the only one who could stop them, which he succeeded in doing around 1178 BCE.

For hundreds of years, the pirates of the Mediterranean continued to harass even the greatest of nations. The slave trade was always the lifeblood of piracy; these seafaring human traffickers would capture people in one country and sell them as slaves to the citizens of another. Ancient Greece fell victim to them with such frequency that a 7th-century hymn describes how a band of pirates, referred to as the Tyrrhenians, captured the Greek god of wine and attempted to sell him into slavery. Dionysus only escaped by turning all of the pirates into dolphins, according to the hymn. Two centuries later, Greece would strike back by fielding some pirates of its own, including a man by the same name as the god of wine, Dionysius the Phocaean, one of the most infamous pirates of all.

These notorious Tyrrhenians may have been Etruscans, the ancient tribe that was, at the same time as the hymns were written, pressuring the citizens of the little town of Rome to form themselves into a kingdom. It would only be in the 3rd century BCE that the Romans themselves, who were now established into the early Roman Republic, would have their first encounter with pirates. Queen Teuta of Illyria (modern-day Balkan Peninsula, including Croatia, Herzegovina, and Bosnia) was following in her late husband's footsteps by attempting to expand her borders. She was one of the first ancient powers to truly invest in piracy as a form of warfare. Her men roamed the Adriatic Sea with instructions to attack and plunder any non-Illyrian vessel that they happened to come across, and so, she created one of the first fleets of buccaneers.

One of Teuta's greatest enemies was the Roman Republic. When Illyrian pirates became a significant problem for Rome, the consul of the time sent out a commander known as Lucius Postumius Albinus, aided by Demetrius of Pharos, to deal with them. Demetrius was an Illyrian and a traitor; his betrayal of Teuta was instrumental in what became known as the First Illyrian War, which lasted from 229 BCE to 228 BCE. Rome won a decisive victory, and the Illyrian pirate problem was solved.

Two hundred years later, Rome still had a pirate problem, except this time, no decisive action would be taken against it. The Tyrrhenians, Illyrians, and Greeks had all been washed away by the tidal wave of time; in their place, the Cilicians had risen up, and these were perhaps the most fearsome of them all.

Cilicia, part of modern-day Turkey, was a relatively new province at the time; Pompey himself would annex it in the 60s BCE. But the pirates that lived there had been terrorizing Rome for much longer than that, and Pompey's conquest of the area would do little to actually stop them. Like the Lukka, who had also inhabited the area, these pirates found it ideal for their illegal operations. The network of coves and little natural bays peppering the shoreline made it easy to conceal ships both from their prey and from those who might try to stop them; there was also an abundance of woods and forests on the shore, making it easy to obtain lumber for building all manner of ships. The pirates themselves were of varying descent, but they all had one thing in common: plunder. The fact that they were not affiliated with any specific country made them more dangerous than any of Teuta's buccaneers. These men were self-serving and wholly independent. They'd cut the throat of any nationality in order to search its pockets.

Like the Tyrrhenians, the Cilician pirates' main focus was on the slave trade, and this was where Rome discovered that these pirates could be useful. Hundreds of thousands of slaves were shipped in from Cilicia to the Roman Republic and sold there; in fact, just as Sicily was Rome's main source of grain, Cilicia became its main source of slaves. This time, there would be no Lucius Postumius Albinus to sally forth and put a stop to slavery. A few half-hearted attempts were made by Marcus Antonius (the grandfather of Mark Antony) to capture Cilicia, but only small portions of the region were ever brought under his control, and even then, the pirates continued with their dastardly work. It was just too convenient to have slaves streaming into the Republic.

The Tyrrhenians might have captured a Greek god, but the Cilicians, in 75 BCE, captured the next best thing: Julius Caesar. Only 25 years old at the time, Caesar was already quick to prove his strategic brilliance, as well as his ruthlessness. The pirates were delighted to have captured a Roman patrician, and instead of selling him into slavery, they decided to post a ransom for him. Caesar was disgusted when he was told that he was being ransomed for only twenty talents of silver. He arrogantly told the pirates that he was worth much more than that, and he bullied them into increasing his ransom to fifty talents of silver.

For the next few weeks, while his associates scrambled to rescue him from the pirate ship, Caesar more or less bossed the pirates around their own ship. He demanded silence while he was sleeping, inserted himself into the pirates' daily activities, and eventually left them with a murderous promise: when his ransom was paid, he was going to have the lot of them crucified. Once freed, Caesar was quick to make good on his promise. He raised a fleet of ships, captured the small island where the pirates were staying, and cut their throats because the proconsul of Asia refused to have them crucified.

The Cilician pirates were about as notorious—both as pirates and as slave traders—as they could be. And to the slaves of Rome, many of whom had passed through their brutal hands and been treated as chattel, they were perhaps even greater enemies than the Romans themselves. That was why it was a tremendous surprise when Spartacus decided to turn to the Cilician pirates for help.

Crassus had been hot on Spartacus' heels ever since their first clash near Picentia. Knowing that he couldn't punch his way through Crassus' army the way he'd done with Publicola and Clodianus, Spartacus continued to move south, and Crassus gleefully pursued, believing that he'd trapped his quarry in Bruttium at last. And it certainly looked that way. Harried by the presence of Crassus, and only a few days ahead of him, Spartacus set up camp at the beginning of 71 BCE on the shores of the Strait of Messina at Rhegium, located at the very southernmost part of Italy. It looked as though he'd been brought to bay, like a treed raccoon with hounds circling the roots.

But Spartacus was not done fighting yet. He had been trapped before, and he had escaped before. The difference was that last time, he had been able to slip away from unwitting guards with the help of 78 others. Now, he had eight Roman legions to face, and he knew that his badly damaged force, which was depleted by the ten thousand who had crossed the Alps and again by the six thousand killed in battle (it's also likely he lost more to disease or cold as well), was not big enough to beat them. He needed reinforcements. And there was only one place left to run to: Sicily.

Sixty years before the time of the Spartacus rebellion, a slave named Eunus had made himself king on the fertile grounds of Sicily, the breadbasket of Italy. The island had always been a place of abundance and agriculture, and where there were farms, there were thousands upon thousands of slaves. Spartacus knew that while he had suffered defeat at the hands of Crassus, he was still a hero in the eyes of the slaves who waited patiently for freedom. If he could make it to Sicily, he would at least have a much more defensible position. He would liberate the slaves there and use them for reinforcements. Even his men would have warm barns to sleep in and more than enough to eat, boosting their morale and their strength. If they could just get to Sicily, they might still have a chance of standing against Crassus.

The only trouble was the Strait of Messina. Nearly three miles wide and eight hundred feet deep, the strait was impassable except by boat. Spartacus had no ships, so there was no way to take tens of thousands of men from the shores of Italy to the abundant fields of Sicily. Taking a military port would be both recklessly ambitious and time-consuming. Roman merchants were steering well clear of the ravaging, ever-hungry rebel army, which had been plundering everywhere it went for years. There was only one option left: the Cilician pirates.

Many of the rebels who now fought in Spartacus' army may have passed through the hands of these cruel human traffickers. Perhaps they remembered swaying in the bellies of those pirate vessels, chained to each other, hopeless in the dark and the sickness and the filth. Once the vessels came ashore, the slaves were dragged out into the sun and stripped naked, then taken to the market with signs hanging around their necks stating their price and other details. They had been poked and prodded by prospective buyers whose eyes ran across their bare bodies with as much respect and dignity as would have been afforded to a piece of furniture. Even a horse was more valuable than most slaves and would have been offered greater care. Then they'd been torn away from the friendships they'd made on those slave ships and sent into new lives, lives of drudgery and abuse, their rights gone, their families forgotten. The Cilician pirates had done this to many of them, and now, Spartacus was turning to them for help. It's likely that the gladiator general faced a fair amount of opposition from his army for this decision, and perhaps rightly so. But Spartacus could see no other way. It was either cross the strait to Sicily on a pirate ship or turn and face the might of eight Roman legions, and he knew that to do so would cause an outright slaughter.

The details have long since been lost to history. Somehow, Spartacus came into contact with a group of the pirates and made a deal with them. Their role was to bring him and all of his men across the strait to Sicily, where, hopefully, their quest for freedom would be renewed. Perhaps Spartacus would even be able to succeed in ruling the island the way Eunus had; it was a poor substitute, in the gladiator's eyes, for going home, but it was better than death. Spartacus had wanted to go back to Thrace, but once again, his hand was being forced by that unrelenting rule that had been presiding over his life ever since he was first captured. *Fight or die.*

We're not sure exactly what Spartacus granted the Cilician pirates in return. He may have offered them a position of power, promising to give them rights to some resources or land in Sicily once he had taken control over the island. It seems more likely, however, that he simply gave them a vast sum of money. Spartacus was not short on money and resources, thanks to the relentless plundering of his army. He probably paid the pirates and then relied on a pirate's honor. Of which, it would soon transpire, there was none.

The day came for the pirates to arrive and load up Spartacus' men to take them to greener pastures. There must have been a buzz in the rebel camp that day, a hint of excitement despite their distrust of the pirates. Instead of being trapped between Crassus and the sea, there was hope now. They were going somewhere that Spartacus had told them was better. They were going to take one step closer to freedom, just as soon as the swift little pirate ships would begin to appear on the horizon, making the waves bristle with masts.

But the ships never came. Whatever payment Spartacus had given them, the pirates had taken it and disappeared to wherever the swift seas would take them. The rebels were on their own.

Chapter 11 – Crassus' Wall

Even the dark cell of Capua had not left Spartacus feeling as securely and completely trapped as he was right now.

The Thracian had achieved so much in the nearly three years since his last time standing in the gladiatorial arena. He'd been a mock hero of entertainment then, killing others like him for the enjoyment of the bloodthirsty crowd. But ever since he and his followers had seized kitchen knives and fled from their prison, he had become something far more. He had become a real hero to real people in a real life-and-death situation. The battles of the gladiators had been staged, even though the spilled blood had been all too real. Yet every drop of Roman blood that stained all of Italy from the Alps to Rhegium had been spilled for a reason, for the sake of freedom, at least in Spartacus' mind. Freedom had been the tantalizing hope that had drawn him every step of the way.

And it was freedom now that he had lost. He might be a real hero to the rebels now, a kind of legend, but he feared that he would never be the one thing he really wanted to be: free. An ordinary Thracian living an ordinary life on the high plateau where he had run and played as a boy. He rued the day that he had become a Roman soldier.

The Cilician pirates had been Spartacus' trump card, his last hope, but now, that hope was gone. Because Crassus had caught up.

It's easy to imagine Crassus practically cackling with glee when he saw the predicament that his worthy adversary had gotten himself into. Spartacus might not have been holed up in a town—or upon the flank of an active volcano—but his position on the peninsula of Bruttium left him almost as vulnerable to a siege as if he had chosen to bring his army into a city. That was, if Crassus could do the impossible: build a wall across the entire peninsula, a wall that would have been forty miles long.

Even as Spartacus scrambled to find a way out, Crassus was busy sealing off his only hope of escape. Crassus' men were driven by a force even more powerful than the hope that Spartacus was offering his people: fear. Knowing that they had to fight or die, they strove to build the enormous wall, complete with a fifteen-foot ditch at the foot of it, in a matter of days.

Spartacus believed the only way to escape was to head toward Sicily. He ordered his men to begin building rafts, made by lashing planks to empty barrels; lumber was cut wherever it could be found, and shipbuilding was attempted. But the rafts were washed out to sea by the fast-flowing waters of the strait, and so, the attempts were abandoned. Some sources claim that Crassus took measures to put a stop to the shipbuilding, although his methods are not described.

Winter came thick and cold that year. The temperatures plummeted, and the balmy summers that had been so good to Spartacus and his men were gone now, reducing fertile Bruttium into what felt like a bare and icy wasteland. Snow fell among the rebel camp and turned to slush, trampled by the feet of men and horses. There were very little provisions left for the men, as Bruttium had already been stripped almost bare, and there was even less grazing for the horses.

Crassus, smug and safe behind his ramparts, knew that he would barely have to fight the rebels at all. Starvation would be his weapon, and he would wield it with a far greater skill than Claudius Glaber had at the feet of Vesuvius.

It was as if the presence of the wall somehow dimmed the golden glow of Spartacus' charisma. Faced with hunger and death, the men had lost hope, and they had lost faith in their leader after his decision to trust the pirates. Cracks began to appear in the cohesion with which Spartacus' men had operated in the early days. The men were hungry, desperate, and terrified. Spartacus knew that it was only their tenacity and fire that had brought them this far, and if he lost those two qualities, then the war would be over. He needed to strike now, hard and fast, not only to gain freedom but to regain morale. It was all they had left.

One night, a snowstorm descended upon the two encamped armies, and Crassus felt a rush of relief and excitement as he watched the white flakes cascade thickly down onto the slumbering landscape. His men had ample food and firewood; the rebels, on the other hand, had been trapped for some time now, and they would have stripped the landscape utterly bare of warmth or sustenance. Surely this snowstorm would be enough to break them. Those left alive in the morning would come crawling to him for surrender, and he would go home to Rome, and the consuls would give him a triumph, and he would finally be on equal footing with Pompey.

Crassus, however, had underestimated one thing about the rebels: their toughness. These were not Roman legionaries who had been given a carefully calculated ration, trained in exactly the right way, or grown up in homes with food and freedom. These men used to be slaves. They were used to being punished for exhaustion by being given more work and less food. They were used to being beaten and starved. They were used to being trapped, and as much as it panicked them, it could not crush them. A mere snowstorm was nothing compared with the icy rage they'd often experienced at the hands of their masters, and so when Spartacus gave one more rousing speech, rallying his army one more time, they rose up and followed him.

None of the Roman legionaries were expecting it when the sound of marching feet among howling snow on the other side of the wall turned out to be the rebel army. Despite being half-blinded by the blizzard, the slaves were attacking. Somehow traversing the massive ditch, they scaled the wall with the same quick agility as they had used rappelling down the cliffs of Mount Vesuvius. Spartacus was leading them personally, and his sword flashed in his hand, snowflakes scattering on his cloaked shoulder, as he struck down one Roman soldier after another. Reinforcements were slow to gather, and by the time the legions could pull themselves together, Spartacus' army was gone: it had melted away into the snowstorm, disappearing but for their tracks. And with the snow coming down fast, even those were almost impossible to follow.

Once again, the rebels had slipped through Crassus' clutches, and Spartacus had access once more to southern Italy. Now perhaps, at last, he could drive north, as hard and as fast as possible, to reach the Alps by the time spring broke and finally break free into the land that he loved and missed. At this point, most classical historians agree that Spartacus' heart was set on nothing but going home. There were many obstacles between the great Thracian and Thrace itself, but at least now he was traveling in the right direction.

But once again, the greatest of those obstacles would prove to be disunity in Spartacus' own ranks. The Germans and Gauls among them—many of them the same men who had followed Crixus in that first fateful split—didn't want to return to Thrace. They still believed that Rome could be conquered, even despite the setbacks they had lately suffered. This time, Spartacus refused to comply with them. He was going north, and if the Germans and Gauls wanted to get themselves killed, then that was their choice. With most of the

Thracians following him, Spartacus kept pushing north, putting distance between himself and the Roman legions.

It was just as well. Crassus had been surprised by the attack in the snowstorm, and he was enraged by the fact that Spartacus had escaped. Terrified of decimation, his troops raced after Spartacus, determined to catch him. Almost demented by jealousy and rage, Crassus was driving them on harder than ever, knowing that it wouldn't be long before Pompey returned.

But they didn't catch up with Spartacus—at least, not at first. Instead, they caught up with the group of Germans and Gauls that Spartacus had left behind. Whether or not they had been expecting tens of thousands of Roman legionaries to come marching down upon them, the group of rebels was not ready to fight them. Even Spartacus knew better than to engage Crassus in a pitched battle; it was why he had attempted his escape in a snowstorm instead of attacking the wall under more favorable conditions. The event that followed was less of a battle than it was a downright disaster. Twelve thousand three hundred rebels perished, cut down mercilessly by the Roman legionaries, and Crassus went on to pursue the rest of Spartacus' army.

Spartacus, meanwhile, had come across the Roman vanguard. It's unspecified how many men were in this vanguard, although the name of its commanding officer is known, a cavalryman named Lucius Quinctius. Quinctius had been attempting to pursue Spartacus ever since he had slipped past him after escaping from the wall, and Spartacus eventually turned back to attack him. This time, with the battle being fought in a series of quick guerrilla movements, Spartacus' army was successful. The vanguard was defeated, and Spartacus and his men were able to keep heading north. Quinctius survived the attack and went on to become a successful politician, but he was never known for his military efforts.

Who knows whether they would have made it, scrambling through Italy as they had done before, all the way back to the Alps? Who knows whether Spartacus might have been able to go home instead of standing by the mountains, like Moses, gazing into the untouchable Promised Land? Perhaps they might have, if they'd been able to keep going. But once again, for reasons unknown, the rebel army came crashing to a halt after the defeat of the Roman vanguard.

Even classical historians could only guess at what caused Spartacus to stop where he did, once again on the very precipice of freedom. Much of it may have had to do with the fact that Spartacus' ragtag rebel army was simply exhausted, incapable of going a step farther after the arduous winter they had suffered. Some historians speculate that the victory over the Roman vanguard had once again gone to the rebels' heads. They may have hoped that all their struggles were merely temporary setbacks and that they could still defeat Crassus if Spartacus would only lead them. Yet most historians agree, and it would appear, that Spartacus himself wanted nothing more than to head back toward the Alps.

Whatever happened, the rebel army came to a halt on the banks of the Silarius River. It is very plausible that the rebels wanted to bring the fight to Crassus, and if that was the case, Spartacus was faced with a terrible choice. Should he do once more what he had done with Crixus, and with the other band of Germans and Gauls, and leave them to the fate they'd chosen? Spartacus could have easily chosen to take a few sympathizers and flee north; the remaining men might have slowed Crassus down long enough for Spartacus, at least, to make his escape. But Crixus had already been killed, and so had the others that Spartacus had left behind. He wouldn't have any more of the rebels' blood on his conscience. So, fatally, Spartacus decided to stay.

As he'd done after the death of Crixus, however, Spartacus committed a dark and ironic act after hearing about the deaths of the 12,300 men. Perhaps in a last bid to dissuade his men from fighting Crassus in open battle, or perhaps simply to fuel their fighting spirit, he ordered that one of the Roman prisoners be brought to him. A cross was made by nailing together two long planks of wood. Then the prisoner, bound and held down, was dragged onto the cross. A single nail was driven through his ankles and into the wood; two more were hammered painfully through the long tendons of his wrists. Blood soaked the wood and ran down his skin, and as he screamed in agony, the rebels hauled the cross upright. And the Roman hung crucified against the gray winter sky, dying slowly and in terrible agony as Spartacus' whole army watched.

Spartacus turned to his troops and told them that if they stayed, if they fought, and if they lost, then this was what would happen to them. They would be crucified, and they would die the ugliest, most painful death imaginable. Crassus would make sure of that.

But the men stayed. And Spartacus was faced one last time with the deadliest choice of all: fight or die.

Chapter 12 – The Last Stand

Illustration IV: The death of Spartacus as imagined by Nicola Sanesi

On the banks of the Silarius, under the shadow of the crucified Roman, Spartacus drew his sword. The gray sky gave it a dull gleam; the blade was scratched and notched, scarred much like the man who wielded it. He stood beside his proud cavalry horse—perhaps the same one they had captured from Varinius, which would have felt like a lifetime ago—and with one swift strike, he killed it. The beautiful animal fell to the ground with a thud that every man in Spartacus' army felt in their bones. He turned to them with hollow eyes, the dark blood of the horse spreading through the iced ground at his feet.

"If we win this battle," he said calmly, "I will have my choice of horses. But if we lose, I will have no more need of a horse."

Spartacus knew that day that he was walking into a battle to the very death. It was the only way he knew how to live: let alone fight or die, he knew he had to win or die. And as Crassus' eight legions waited for the rebels with a quiet patience that nonetheless hummed with power, Spartacus knew that there was no way he could win. The fools who loved him, who followed him, had made one mistake too many. They should have crossed the Alps a year ago.

But they hadn't. They were here now, facing the Roman legions in a pitched battle, and there was nothing that Spartacus could do about it. Ever since breaking through the ramparts, Spartacus knew he had been steadily losing control over his men. The sight of Crassus' army showing up and setting itself in array against the rebels had already caused several small groups of rebels to break off from the main army and attack Crassus without Spartacus' command, always ending in tragedy.

Even Spartacus had, for the first time, considered that there might be an option other than to fight or die. He sent messengers to Crassus, hoping to make peace with his enemy; the Roman army, for all its might, had also suffered much that winter, and Spartacus hoped that Crassus would opt for a quick peace. But the Roman's goal was not to make peace. It was to gain glory, and even though making a truce with Spartacus could have saved thousands of lives, Crassus wasn't interested in conserving human life—as he had clearly demonstrated in his decimation of the troops. He was interested in winning, in being as glorious and as praised and admired as Pompey. And the only way that was going to happen was if he utterly defeated and annihilated the wily Thracian who faced him.

Crassus was also aware that Pompey had already returned to Rome; in fact, the Senate had sent him and his war-hardened legions straight toward Bruttium. As Crassus prepared for battle with Spartacus, Pompey was already on his way. If the richest man in Rome was going to get his glorious military victory, he had to do it quickly, before Pompey reached them and claimed the glory for ending the war.

So, Spartacus was truly out of options. There would be no more surprise attacks on Crassus, no more guerilla warfare. There was only one thing left to do, and it was the last thing that Spartacus wanted: a pitched battle. He hoped that by using two grisly actions— the crucifixion of the Roman and the killing of his horse—he would inspire the rebels as well as he could. It felt like a last resort.

And then he charged into battle.

On foot, sword in his hand, Spartacus rushed forth, and the tidal wave of the rebels (what was left of them, anyway) came crashing after him. Spartacus headed for one particular spot in the line, the place where Crassus himself was standing, surrounded by centurions. In those moments, all that Spartacus could think of was his hatred. Hatred for this man who'd turned the tide of a war that had looked so promising. Hatred for this pompous Roman, a man who already had everything that Spartacus had ever dreamed of, a home, a family, a wife, the freedom to do and become whatever he wanted, the freedom to be wherever he wanted. But it hadn't been enough for Crassus. The basic rights that Spartacus had been fighting for weren't enough for him. Not even his overwhelming wealth was enough for him, wealth that gave him the freedom to do as he pleased. No, Crassus needed glory, too, and because of his need for praise and admiration, because of his arrogance, Spartacus wasn't ever going to go home. He knew it deep down. But maybe, if he fought hard enough, he'd give Crassus what he deserved—a death at the edge of a sword.

All around Spartacus, the sounds of battle dissolved into a fog of madness and fear. There were clashes and screams, feet and hooves thundering and churning on the icy earth. Armor and weapons flashed at him as he continued his charge, and he shoved them all aside, even when the hot blood of his own comrades sprayed against his face. He made straight for Crassus, for the centurions surrounding him, fighting with that desperation that had kept him alive in the gladiatorial arena.

Maybe Spartacus believed that if he killed Crassus, the Roman troops would realize they had no one left to fear. Maybe they'd give up, and he could go free after all. Either way, it was with desperation and rage that he finally reached the centurions guarding Crassus and crossed blades with them. The legions began to close in around Spartacus and the men nearest him, but he fought on, slashing and stabbing, turning and striking, a whirlwind of rage and death, and the centurions' blood splashed on his armor. He killed two of them, and then there was nothing standing between him and Crassus. The courageous gladiator and the jealous praetor faced each other for an instant, and Spartacus was ready to strike.

But Spartacus and Crassus, by all accounts, would never actually exchange blows. Instead, one of the other Romans struck first. He slashed Spartacus in the leg, opening an ugly wound that poured blood onto the icy ground. The rebel leader fell to his knees, unable to rise, but he still refused to surrender. Striking upward at the wave of enemies that kept on coming at him, he killed several more

Roman soldiers before they were everywhere, butchering his men and surrounding him. And even then, he fought to his last movement, to his last strike.

To the last beat of his heart.

The Battle of the Silarius River, fought on an unknown date in early 71 BCE, was less of a battle than it was simply a massacre. Only one thousand Romans perished, while Spartacus' force was utterly destroyed. Some of the rebels escaped into the mountains, but the vast majority of them were killed in numbers so great that their corpses lay strewn everywhere on the battlefield. One of those corpses belonged to Spartacus. The road from Capua, for all his courage and brilliance, had led him to a mass grave in Italy. He would never see Thrace again. Not even his bones would rest under Thracian stars, as Spartacus' body was never even identified. Along with the thousands of his fellow rebels—the men he'd refused to leave behind, the men he'd fought and died for—he was cast into a mass grave and forgotten. The grave still lies unmarked somewhere at the mouth of the modern-day Sele River. He was only around forty years old when he died.

The bones of one of the world's greatest heroes rotted away among the corpses of his followers, beneath the spot where he had both fought and died.

Chapter 13 – Aftermath

The Third Servile War was over, and Spartacus was dead. But even for Marcus Licinius Crassus, this could hardly be counted as a victory.

Oh, the Romans won, that much was indisputable. The rebels were not so much defeated as they were simply slaughtered. It's also difficult to imagine how it would have been done without Crassus' brutal yet effective command. The disunity in Spartacus' ranks certainly contributed to the problem, but Crassus, savage as he was, was the only commander who took Spartacus seriously enough that he could finally be forced into pitched battle and defeated.

But as far as Crassus was concerned, the victory came just a little too late. The battle was likely still in full swing when suddenly the horizon was covered in red and silver. Legionaries came marching in by the thousands, their strong rectangular shields held up, their ranks bristling with spears like the quills on a gigantic porcupine. It was Pompey. He'd arrived from Rome just in time, according to him, to save the day. Crassus' legions had left only small groups of scattered rebels, and Pompey busily set to work cleaning them up. The exhausted and battered ranks of Crassus' army had done the bulk of the work, and Crassus knew he had been the commander who ended the Third Servile War. But once again, Pompey arrived to steal the glory right out from under his nose.

Pompey captured thousands of rebels. They were without their leader now, scattered in ragged bunches everywhere, no longer even attempting to fight the Romans. For three glorious years, these men had been rebels. But the loss of Spartacus had reduced them to panicked sheep without a shepherd; they weren't rebels or revolutionaries anymore. They were just escaped slaves, lost and terrified, and they were cut down in the thousands by Pompey's troops. Most of them were fleeing north, back toward Capua along the Appian Way, which is perhaps ironic considering that it was at Capua that the war truly started. Seventy-eight men had fled from there with kitchen knives in 73 BCE. Now, six thousand men were fleeing back in that direction, pursued by hostile Romans.

And they were captured. And once they were captured, these slaves were not returned to their owners. Pompey and Crassus both knew that an example would have to be made out of them. The stories about the Spartacus rebellion had sparked unrest among the still-captive slaves all across the Roman Republic, and there were so many of them that if all of those slaves decided to rise up—if another Spartacus appeared to lead them—then they could possibly outnumber their masters and overwhelm them. This was the third servile war in less than a hundred years, and Pompey decided that this time, it would be the last. He would make an example out of these rebels, an example so brutal that it would put any thoughts of rebellion to death.

So, he crucified them. Just as Spartacus thought would happen.

And it was not just one or two of the prisoners. No, Pompey crucified every single man and woman that he captured, lining the length of the Appian Way with wooden crosses and struggling, gasping, dying rebels. All the way from Rome to Brindisi, the great road was flanked by gory death. The Romans left them there to die—sometimes it took days—as they went on to pursue more of the rebels. When they caught them, the Romans would bring them back to the Appian Way, nail them to the wooden crosses, and hoist them into the air. Hanging from the nail holes in their hands, forced to brace themselves against the nail in their ankles to be able to lift their chests and breathe, these men suffered horrifically for hours upon hours until they finally died from asphyxiation or, sometimes, sheer exhaustion. All who passed along the Appian Way saw their naked corpses hanging there, some of them still breathing, some screaming, but their eyes all lifeless with suffering. They had hoped for freedom, but what they gained was a slow and agonizing death.

Six thousand rebels were crucified along that road during the beginning of 71 BCE. And their six thousand bodies were left to hang on the crosses until the bodies rotted away. The seasons came and went, and the skeletons were bleached white, as the wind rattled them and blew through the empty ribcages, singing mournfully to the slaves of the Roman Republic that freedom was nothing but a dream. A foolish, deadly dream.

They lined the road from Capua to Rome like a ghostly honor guard for their dead general. And Pompey's plan worked: there would never be a servile war in Rome again.

As for the gladiatorial games, their time was just beginning. They would only reach the height of their popularity almost five hundred years later, where thousands of them would fight each other at a time for the enjoyment of the masses. They were finally stopped by Emperor Honorius in 404 CE.

* * *

Crassus never got the triumph that he dreamed of. Just as he had expected, Pompey was given all of the credit for ending the Third Servile War. Yet another glorious triumph was thrown across the streets of Rome for him, and the crowds sang his praises as he rode in a chariot like modern-day royalty. Crassus was given only a motley little ovation—a simple parade on foot through a small section of Rome. And while it was still a significant honor, it planted a seed of blazing hatred in Crassus' heart. He had been the one who did all the work of putting down the Spartacus rebellion, and he knew it. Pompey's role in the war had simply been that of chasing down a few remaining rebel elements. Crassus had whipped all of those legions into shape, led them against Spartacus, built a forty-mile wall to lay siege to an entire peninsula, and even decimated his own army in order to defeat the gladiator general. Yet, even so, he was given almost no military recognition. The people of Rome still viewed Spartacus' rebellion as something of an embarrassment, especially now that the actual threat had faded from their memories. Defeating Sertorius in Spain held much greater prestige, and Pompey was hailed as a hero, while Crassus was barely recognized at all. Crassus tried to make up for this with a series of lavish celebratory banquets, but he never gained the title of "Great" that Pompey carried.

The frustration and ignominy resulting from this lack of recognition would pursue Crassus for the rest of his life, never allowing him to rest from the black shadow of jealousy that nipped at his heels. All through his life, he would continue to compete with Pompey for popularity and prestige, and he would never quite win.

In 70 BCE, both Crassus and Pompey were elected as consuls. They were forced to work together, which they did begrudgingly, making numerous political reforms and weeding corruption out of the Senate. Crassus appears to have been a fairly able consul, but he just couldn't compare with Pompey in the following years. Where his illustrious rival set off on military conquests, Crassus was elected as a censor, a task at which he failed miserably. He was sent to annex Egypt and, when he proved incapable of doing so, he was removed from his position.

Pompey, meanwhile, was tasked with finally weeding out the Cilician pirates once and for all. These pirates had been terrorizing Rome for decades, and putting a stop to their activities took Pompey only three months. In fact, Pompey was able to relocate the pirates to more inland towns, where most of them were integrated into productive society and lived peaceful lives as farmers. He followed that up by heading toward Armenia, where he conquered Tigranes the Great and helped to end the last of the Mithridatic Wars. He became the darling of Rome, its leading military hero. Crassus' defeat of Spartacus was all but forgotten.

Even his political career appeared to be almost over thanks to his bumbling failure as a censor. He had, however, formed an alliance in the late 60s BCE with a young man who would prove to be more legendary than Pompey, Crassus, and Spartacus put together: Julius Caesar. None the worse off for his encounter with the Cilician pirates, Caesar was angling to become a consul, and Crassus and Pompey both worked together to back him. When he was elected in 59 BCE, his alliances with Crassus and Pompey resulted in the First Triumvirate. The Roman Republic was dying, and Crassus was now one of the leading figures in its swansong.

Crassus' wealth was, by this point, almost impossibly huge. He was also one of the three most powerful men in Rome. But he still hadn't proven himself on the battlefield, and his wealth and power were nothing to him without fame and popularity. As a part of the Triumvirate, he was sent to Syria as its governor, and it was here that he was finally given an opportunity to prove himself once more.

Rome had been at war with Parthia—modern-day Iran—for decades. And Crassus jumped at the chance to go to battle with the Parthian king, Orodes II. 54 BCE proved to be a good year for Crassus' campaign; he pushed Orodes out of Armenia and seemed to be finally winning the war. If he could end the war with Parthia, he would be given even greater glory than Pompey could ever achieve.

But he didn't. Crassus grew overambitious, blinded by his quest for greatness. He launched a daring attack into the heart of Parthia itself without enough men, even though his son had already been killed in battle and the Armenian king, a former Roman ally, had deserted them. Now well into middle age, Crassus was no longer the commander that he had been when he was fighting the Third Servile War almost twenty years ago. He led his legions right into the range of Orodes II's swift horseback archers, who were more than a match for the lumbering Romans. Quickly surrounding the Romans, Orodes' archers subjected them to a rain of arrows so thick that the legionaries could barely see. Those left alive were forced to surrender, not only their weapons but also their banner.

Losing their banner was a disgrace even greater than throwing down one's weapons in flight. For Crassus, it was an unbearable humiliation. Perhaps he would have found some sense of relief in the fact that he wouldn't be able to go back to Rome and face the degradation of those whose admiration he sought so fiercely. Crassus would never set foot in his city or spend a single aureus of his wealth ever again because Orodes killed him in 53 BCE. Legend has it that he had liquid gold poured down his throat so that he suffocated and burned in the metal for which he'd made so many corrupt choices. It's more likely that he was executed or just plain killed in battle, though.

Either way, Crassus would never become the hero he wanted to be. And shortly afterward, it was Pompey himself who would march across Armenia and conquer the Parthians, cleaning up Crassus' mess one last time.

Chapter 14 – Legacy

ustration V: The Bolshoi Ballet depicts Spartacus in chains

"In overthrowing me, you have cut down only the trunk of the Tree of Liberty." The words were delivered through gritted teeth, his brown eyes blazing with defiance. "It will spring up again by the roots for they are numerous and deep."

These words, uttered by Toussaint L'Ouverture (also spelled as Louverture) of Saint Domingue, were as prophetic as they were defiant. The revolutionary and former slave had risen up in 1791, inspired by the French Revolution, to overthrow the Frenchmen who had dominion over him and his brothers. The French Revolution had come and gone, but the revolution in Saint Domingue continued on, freeing half a million slaves as they overthrew the French, the British, and the Spanish. And this man, this defiant black man who dared to spit in the eye of Napoleon himself, had led it. In fact, where he stood now before Napoleon, Toussaint L'Ouverture was the governor-general of both Saint Domingue—later to be named Haiti—and Hispaniola, the modern-day Dominican Republic.

L'Ouverture had led the only successful slave revolt in modern history. It was thanks to the fact that slaves outnumbered free people ten to one on the island, and also to L'Ouverture's excellent military command, that all three of the great empires that had come to fight him had been defeated. The British had died of yellow fever, the French had succumbed in battle, and the Spanish had been unable to keep L'Ouverture out of Hispaniola. The man was unstoppable, but so was Napoleon. And it was Napoleon who stopped him. L'Ouverture would die of pneumonia in a French prison in 1803. His jailer refused to allow physicians near him, saying that because he was black, and therefore wholly different, the European doctors wouldn't know how to treat him.

The revolution, however, did not die with L'Ouverture. It lived on beyond him, just as he had prophesied. On New Year's Day, 1804, Haiti became an independent country. France begrudgingly recognized its independence. This came sixty years before the American Civil War would put an end to slavery in the United States of America, and it came one hundred years before Cuba would throw off its Spanish shackles and declare equality and freedom. Haiti was one of the first, and L'Ouverture led it into the dawn of freedom.

For that reason, they called him the "Black Spartacus."

* * *

Toussaint L'Ouverture was not the only man to invoke the name of Spartacus in his quest for freedom. To this day, the gladiator general has left a legacy of courage and sacrifice in the name of freedom that has lived on in historical events and popular culture alike.

Karl Marx was one of Spartacus' great fans; his later revolutionary admirer, Che Guevara, would also see Spartacus as a hero. Guevara was an important part of the Cuban Revolution, an event that would change the course of history not only in Cuba but also in the rest of the world, as it placed communist leader Fidel Castro in charge of the island, which is located just ninety miles from Florida. Spartacus had been dead for a little over two thousand years, but he was still hailed as a hero by those who saw themselves as fighting for freedom against an arrogant aristocracy; in the case of the Cuban Revolution, corrupt President Fulgencio Batista was an ideal—and eerie—echo of rich and jealous Crassus.

Guevara was not the only Marxist to proclaim himself to be a follower of the long-dead Spartacus. In post-WWI Germany, the so-called Spartacist Revolt caused chaos in Berlin in January 1919. After the abdication of Kaiser Wilhelm II after World War I ended in defeat for Germany, a socialist republic was founded, and Marxist leaders Karl Liebknecht and Rosa Luxemburg decided to try and tip the scales toward full-blown communism. Liebknecht and Luxemburg had suffered during the First World War, and both ended up in prison shortly thereafter, having been arrested for treason in 1916. Upon their release two years later, they formed what they called the Spartacist League. Like Guevara and Castro, they saw communism as a solution for oppression by an aristocratic minority, and they named themselves after the famed gladiator general with visions of freedom.

Sadly, for Liebknecht and Luxemburg, their bid for what they perceived as freedom would be just as unsuccessful as that of Spartacus. Although their revolt succeeded in capturing numerous important buildings in Berlin, their supporters were ultimately no match for the German military. Hundreds of Spartacists were shot and killed; many of these were in an execution-style after the revolutionaries had already laid down their weapons. Liebknecht was shot. Luxemburg had her skull bashed in and was cast into the river by a bunch of derisive soldiers. Germany freed itself from the clutches of communism and attempted to establish a democracy, but of course, the worst was yet to come for this country. Hitler and the Nazis were on their way.

Not all of the events inspired by Spartacus were grim ones, however. Although the German Spartacists were not the last to call themselves by that name—there were groups in the United States and the United Kingdom with similar ethos who also called themselves Spartacists in the 1970s—Spartacus' legacy lives on in popular culture as well. The courageous story of a gladiator who tried to overthrow an entire government still captures the imagination of the world.

Perhaps the earliest writer to create a work of fiction based on Spartacus' extraordinary life was Raffaello Giovagnoli with his 1874 novel, *Spartacus*. Many more would follow: Arthur Koestler's *The Gladiators*, Lewis Grassic Gibbon's *Spartacus*, and Halina Rudnicka's *The Students of Spartacus*.

In 1960, Stanley Kubrick's film *Spartacus* embellished the story, but it nonetheless brought this piece of history to life on the big screen for the first time. It was the recipient of an Academy Award and also created the famous "I'm Spartacus!" quote. As rousing as the scene may have been, there is sadly no historical evidence to support the story of hundreds of Spartacus' followers rising up to prevent their leader's capture.

Spartacus' tale would also inspire a ballet, which was composed in 1956 by Aram Khachaturian, an Armenian. The ballet was based on Giovagnoli's novel, but like the novel, its ties to real events were strong ones. Khachaturian's words about the ballet perhaps best summarize how Spartacus' story has influenced both history and culture throughout the two thousand years following his failed rebellion. "I thought of *Spartacus* as a monumental fresco describing the mighty avalanche of the antique rebellion of slaves on behalf of human rights...When I composed the score of the ballet and tried to capture the atmosphere of ancient Rome in order to bring to life the images of the remote past, I never ceased to feel the spiritual affinity of Spartacus to our own time."

Spiritual or not, for centuries, the struggle of Spartacus has been one that the modern world has had an affinity with, and for good reason. Spartacus' rebellion might not have been about abolition, but it was still about freedom. It was still about struggling out of the clutches of a powerful enemy. Spartacus might not have been dreaming about a Roman Republic where no one would ever be enslaved again. But he was dreaming about walking free under the Thracian stars. He was dreaming of going home, and at the very heart of all struggles for human rights, home and freedom are still their themes.

Conclusion

Slavery would only end in the Roman Empire when it gradually faded out of existence during the latter years of the Empire, but even then, it eventually turned into serfdom, which was barely any better. All across the world, for thousands of years to follow, slaves would continue to fight for their freedom. Many simply fought to escape slavery, like Spartacus and his men did. But in later years, freedom fighters would rise up who sought to abolish slavery altogether.

Slavery did not die with the Roman Empire. Throughout the Middle Ages, slaves were still common throughout most of the world. In Europe, slavery was largely replaced with the feudal system, in which serfs worked for free and had their lives generally controlled by their lords—a kind of bondage hardly better than slavery itself.

The discovery of the Americas and the colonization of Africa brought about slavery on a scale that ancient Rome could never even have dreamed of. When Portuguese traders began the transatlantic slave trade in 1444, they ushered in an era of the most horrific exploitation of man by his own fellow man that the world has ever seen. The transatlantic slave trade would rip around 12.5 million

African people from the country where they'd grown up, forcibly relocate them to the New World, and put them to work in countries that were filled with peril. From abusive masters to diseases for which they had no immunity, those slaves who lived long enough to reach the New World lived appalling and dangerous lives. The tide only began to turn in 1781, which was when slavery was first abolished in the Holy Roman Empire. The French Revolution (and the subsequent Haitian Revolution) in the late 18th and early 19th centuries were fuel to the flame of abolition.

It was only in 1848, however, that one of the prominent colonial powers would abolish slavery in all of its New World colonies. Ironically, considering it was a French emperor who killed L'Ouverture, this power was France during its Second Republic. Spain, Great Britain, and the United States reluctantly followed. Finally, in 1888, slavery in the New World mostly ended when the Golden Law was passed, abolishing slavery in South America.

In the modern day, slavery is finally illegal in every recognized country across the globe. That's not to say it doesn't exist anymore, however. Twenty-one million people—almost twice the number that crossed the Atlantic Ocean on slave ships—are still living in some form of slavery. Child trafficking, forced labor, bonded labor, and forced marriage are only some of the ways in which millions of people all over the world are still being exploited as slaves. Fifty-five percent of these are women, and about twenty-five percent are children.

The atrocity lives on. But it no longer dares to walk in the sunlight. Spartacus was only the first in a long line of heroes who continue to campaign bravely against this dark monster, this disgusting atrocity against humanity. Toussaint L'Ouverture, Frederick Douglass, Abraham Lincoln, Olaudah Equiano, William Wilberforce—their names ring down through the distance of the centuries as those who dared to stand against that monster. And Spartacus was their leader, the first of them all.

This courageous Roman gladiator may not have planned to abolish slavery. The very concept of abolition would have been an utterly foreign one to him; the Roman economy and culture were so deeply entrenched in the practice of slavery that the absence of slavery was almost inconceivable.

Spartacus didn't make lengthy speeches about human rights. In fact, human rights weren't even something that people thought about in the Roman Republic. But he did know the struggle for freedom that so many great men and women would share in during later centuries. He knew, perhaps not as intellectually as Abraham Lincoln or Harriet Tubman, that the exploitation of one human being by another was wrong, painful, and cruel. He knew that he didn't want to spend the rest of his life shackled in a Roman cell. He knew that the sound of the wind across the Thracian plateau called him even when that plateau was so far away. And he knew that the tens of thousands— the 120,000, at one point—who followed him also deserved to walk as free men.

He gave his life fighting for a free world. And almost 2,100 years later, courageous individuals still follow in his footsteps, believing in hope. Believing in freedom.

Check out another book by Captivating History

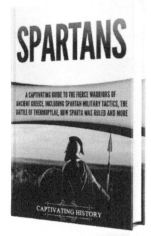

Sources

Anti-slavery charities to support today:

Anti-Slavery International: https://antislavery.org/

Polaris Project: www.polarisproject.org

Prajwala: www.prajwalaindia.com

Children's Organization of Southeast Asia: www.cosaasia.org

Urban Light: www.urban-light.org

GoodWeave: www.goodweave.org

The Empower Foundation: www.empowerfoundation.org

To learn more about modern-day slavery and how you can help, visit http://www.thedailymuse.com/education/human-trafficking-the-myths-and-the-realities/

Quantum Future Group 2016, *Event 74: Second Servile War; Gaius Marius*, Quantum Future Group: The Chronicle of the Fall of the Roman Empire, viewed 23 December 2019, <https://cof.quantumfuturegroup.org/events/74>

Cartwright, M. 2013, *Slavery in the Roman World*, Ancient History Encyclopedia, viewed 23 December 2019, <http://libraryguides.vu.edu.au/harvard/internet-websites>

"Ancient Roman Slaves: A Life of Bondage" History on the Net © 2000-2019, Salem Media.
December 23, 2019 <https://www.historyonthenet.com/ancient-roman-slaves>

Simkin, J. 1997, *Slavery in the Roman Empire*, Spartacus Educational, viewed 23 December 2019, <https://spartacus-educational.com/ROMslaves.htm>

Violatti, C. 2016, *10 Interesting Facts About Slavery in the Roman Empire*, Listverse, viewed 23 December 2019, <https://listverse.com/2016/06/05/10-interesting-facts-about-slavery-in-ancient-rome/>

Editors of Encyclopedia Britannica, 2008, *Lucius Cornelius Cinna,* Encyclopedia Britannica, viewed 27 December 2019, <https://www.britannica.com/biography/Lucius-Cornelius-Cinna>

Wilmott, T. 2013, *Gladiators in Ancient Rome: How did they live and die?,* BBC History Magazine, viewed 30 December 2019, <https://www.historyextra.com/period/roman/gladiators-in-ancient-rome-how-did-they-live-and-die/>

Cartwright, M. 2019, *Roman Gladiator*, Ancient History Encyclopedia, viewed 30 December 2019, <https://www.ancient.eu/gladiator/>

Gill, N.S. "Roman Gladiators." ThoughtCo. https://www.thoughtco.com/roman-gladiators-overview-120901 (accessed December 30, 2019).

Andrews, E. 2018, *10 Things You May Not Know About Roman Gladiators*, History, viewed 30 December 2019, <https://www.history.com/news/10-things-you-may-not-know-about-roman-gladiators>

Rickard, J (14 September 2017), SULLA'S SECOND CIVIL WAR, 83-82 BC, http://www.historyofwar.org/articles/wars_sullas_second_civil_war.html

Rickard, J (30 March 2018), l. Cornelius cinna (d.84 bc), http://www.historyofwar.org/articles/people_cinna.html

Editors of encyclopedia Britannica 2019, praetor, encyclopedia Britannica, viewed 30 December 2019, <https://www.britannica.com/topic/praetor>

Hughes, t. 2017, Sertorius: how one man took on an empire, battles of the ancients, viewed 30 December 2019, <http://turningpointsoftheancientworld.com/index.php/2017/07/24/sertorius-hispania-sucro-river/>

Mclaughlin, w. 2016, Battle of Mount VesuviusS spartacus and his men rappelling down a mountain, war history online, viewed 30 December 2019, <https://www.warhistoryonline.com/ancient-history/battle-mount-vesuvius-spartacus-men-rapelling-mountain.html>

Lendering, J. 2019, *Decimation*, Livius, viewed 31 December 2019, <https://www.livius.org/articles/concept/decimation/>

Military History Now 2014, *Removal of a Tenth: A Brief and Bloody History of Decimation*, Military History Now.com, viewed 31 December 2019, <https://militaryhistorynow.com/2014/02/26/no-safety-in-numbers-a-brief-history-of-decimation/>

Strauss, B., *The Spartacus War*, Simon and Schuster 2009

Dimuro, G. 2019, *Crixus: Spartacus' Right-Hand Man Who May Have Been the Gladiator Army's Downfall*, All That's Interesting, viewed 31 December 2019, <https://allthatsinteresting.com/crixus>

Know the Romans, *Roman Weapons & Armor*, viewed 2 January 2020, <https://www.knowtheromans.co.uk/Categories/RomanArmy/RomanWeaponsandArmour/>

Ward, C. O., *The Ancient Lowly*, Рипол Классик 1970

Lendering, J. 2019, *Thracians*, Livius, viewed 2 January 2020, <https://www.livius.org/articles/people/thracians/#Roman%20Conquest>

Mark, J. J. 2019, *Pirates of the Mediterranean,* Ancient History Encyclopedia, viewed 7 January 2020, <https://www.ancient.eu/article/47/pirates-of-the-mediterranean/>

Lendering, J. 2019, *Cilician Pirates*, Livius, viewed 7 January 2020, <https://www.livius.org/articles/people/cilician-pirates/>

Wasson, D. L. 2014, *Spartacus*, Ancient History Encyclopedia, viewed during December 2019, <https://www.ancient.eu/spartacus/>

Czech, K. P. 1994, *Spartacus: The Grecian Slave Warrior who Threatened Rome,* Military History Magazine, viewed during December 2019, <https://www.historynet.com/spartacus-the-grecian-slave-warrior-who-threatened-rome.htm>

Cartwright, M. 2013, *Marcus Licinius Crassus*, Ancient History Encyclopedia, viewed during December 2019, <https://www.ancient.eu/Marcus_Licinius_Crassus/>

Freidani, A. 2019, *Money was not enough for Crassus, the richest man in Rome*, National Geographic, viewed during December 2019, <https://www.nationalgeographic.com/history/magazine/2019/05-06/crassus-romes-richest-man/>

Mark, J. J. 2016, *The Spartacus Revolt*, Ancient History Encyclopedia, viewed during December 2019, <https://www.ancient.eu/article/871/the-spartacus-revolt/>

Lendering, J. 2019, *Spartacus*, Livius, viewed during December 2019, <https://www.livius.org/articles/person/spartacus/>

Gill, N. S. 2019, *Biography of Spartacus, a Slave Who Led a Revolt*, ThoughtCo, viewed during December 2019, <https://www.thoughtco.com/who-was-spartacus-112745>

Editors of Encyclopedia Britannica, *Third Servile War*, Encyclopedia Britannica, viewed 7 January 2020, <https://www.britannica.com/event/Gladiatorial-War>

Sutherland, C. 2007, *Haitian Revolution (1791-1804),* Black Past, viewed 7 January 2020, <https://www.blackpast.org/global-african-history/haitian-revolution-1791-1804/>

Thomson, I. 2004, *The Black Spartacus*, The Guardian, viewed 7 January 2020, <https://www.theguardian.com/books/2004/jan/31/featuresreviews.guardianreview35>

Cavendish, R. 2009, *The Spartacist Uprising in Berlin*, History Today, viewed 7 January 2020, <https://www.historytoday.com/archive/spartacist-uprising-berlin>

Schwarm, B., *Spartacus*, Encyclopedia Britannica, viewed 7 January 2020, <https://www.britannica.com/topic/Spartacus-ballet-by-Khachaturian>

Kelly, A. 2013, *Modern-day Slavery: An Explainer*, The Guardian, viewed 7 January 2020, <https://www.theguardian.com/global-development/2013/apr/03/modern-day-slavery-explainer>

Illustration I:
https://commons.wikimedia.org/wiki/File:Marcus_Licinius_Crassus.jpg

Illustration II:
https://commons.wikimedia.org/wiki/File:3rd_servile_72_plutarch.png

Illustration III:
https://commons.wikimedia.org/wiki/File:Marmolada,_Italy.jpg

Illustration IV:
https://commons.wikimedia.org/wiki/File:Spartacus_by_Sanesi.jpg

Illustration V: By Bengt Nyman - Flickr: DSC_9865, CC BY 2.0, https://commons.wikimedia.org/w/index.php?curid=30261808

Made in the USA
Coppell, TX
06 December 2021

67382837R00069